# Love Lifted Me

### Revised edition including
### "Autumn Years' Reflections"

## Charles F. Geddes

**JOHN RITCHIE LTD**
CHRISTIAN PUBLICATIONS

40 Beansburn, Kilmarnock, Scotland

ISBN-13: 978 1 907731 12 9

www.ritchiechristianmedia.co.uk

Typeset by John Ritchie Ltd., Kilmarnock
Printed by Bell & Bain Ltd., Glasgow

# Contents

Charles and Grace Geddes on their Golden Wedding Day

# The Author
## Charles F. Geddes

As a young child Charles Geddes was abandoned by his parents. He was reared by grandparents in the most squalid of conditions and in a most superstitious atmosphere. Deprivation led to all forms of "hang-ups" which led to the development of a most aggressive personality. This reached a climax when a runaway episode led to further and complete rejection by his parents.

Fortunately, his aggression was channelled into the sport of boxing, which, along with playing in a dance-band, became his whole life. Discontentment, however, caused him to seek for some meaning to life. The story is really about the searching for meaning and understanding of life.

After initial set-backs he finally came face to face with the reality of God. A personal encounter with the Jesus of the Cross transformed his whole life (and that of his home). In spite of all the disadvantages of early deprivation and physical handicaps, he entered College and graduated with a degree in three subjects. He then taught Religious Education in various schools in the north of Scotland.

He and his wife Grace went on to serve the Lord in the West Indies as full-time missionaries.

# Dedications

To my dear partner in life, Grace, "Many daughters have done virtuously, but thou excellest them all" (Proverbs 31:29).

To the late Ian Condie, a "brother and companion in tribulation" who reached out the hand of friendship when it was needed most.

# Preface

I started this little volume some time ago but the inevitable use of the ugly personal pronoun 'I' forced me to lay it aside with no desire to complete it. The last thing I wanted to do was to give anyone the impression that I had an inflated conception of my own importance. When the 'Listening' magazine in Canada, however, kindly published a short account of my testimony, I was surprised and delighted to hear from people in various parts of the world who had been blessed of the Lord in the reading of it, and some indeed made specific requests for a more detailed account.

I then felt that if the Lord could be exalted, sinners challenged, and saints encouraged by my humble story, then this volume would justify its existence. I trust that my 'academic' friends will see beyond the glaring lack of literary merit, and feel the pulse of sincerity behind every word and expression. What I have tried to write about is really "Better felt than telt".

I wish to correct a slight error in relation to my story in the *Listening* magazine. After going into the matter more carefully with relatives, I've learned that only four of us were abandoned as children and not five as stated, (the fifth child was due but had not actually been born at that time).

# Foreword

Many success stories are being told today, particularly connected with business enterprise, inventive achievement, financial wizardry and popular entertainment — all very colourful and sensational. This autobiography, however, does not attempt to compete for a rating with any of them. IT IS a real success story, simply and humbly told by the author himself, not for self-praise, but with a genuine desire to help all who are faced with seemingly insurmountable barriers, to overcome and enjoy a life of fulfilment and purpose.

Everything seemed against him from birth. A split-up, unhappy family relationship, a very humble poverty-stricken upbringing, and in adolescence a distressing disease, all combined to crush this young life. By sheer grit and determination he overcame every disadvantage.

The first half of the story graphically describes the traditional culture and life-style of the fishing communities around the Scottish Moray Firth. The author, in his boyhood, was observing the passing of an era — the first half of this century, with its hardships, tragedies and bravery as far as the fisher-folk were concerned. Although local phrases and dialect are woven through the story and may be strange to some readers, they are well worth preserving in this book.

The story has a Before and an After. The pivotal point was his personal experience with God, but I will not anticipate how the reader will react to the challenge of this, save to say that "It is no secret what God can do".

I heartily recommend this volume to young and old with the words of another:

"Have you got any rivers which you think are uncrossable?
Got any mountains you can't tunnel through?
God specialises in things thought impossible,
He can do anything you cannot do."

Angus Swanson.

# Chapter 1

## THE IDOLS BURIED

"See you later then."

Grannie's care-worn face broke into a toothless smile in assent as I lifted a rather shapeless parcel from the worm-eaten sideboard. In front of her armchair a fire roared in the old-fashioned grate. Above her head a gas-mantle glowed, causing the long polished brass rod on the dark, blistered mantelshelf to gleam. Tucking the bundle under my arm I stepped out into the darkness of a cold wintry night.

As an amateur boxer I had acquired an impressive collection of trophies, and they had meant everything to me. They had been given pride of place in a display cabinet in my bedroom. Now they had been taken from the shelves, wrapped in an old sheet of brown paper and roughly tied with string.

The icy wind blowing in from the Moray Firth could not quench the joy that welled up in my heart as I walked alone in the direction of the Buckie harbour. Indeed the previous ten months had been the happiest in my whole life. Such was my new joy that I had been given to sudden outbursts of lusty singing as I worked on the building-site, much to the annoyance of my workmates. I smiled to myself as I considered that the real cause of their criticism wasn't so much my lack of singing talent, but my limited repertoire, which consisted only of hymns and choruses. "Love Lifted Me" was my favourite, for it had a lot to do with the happiness that had come into my life.

The sea sounded in a menacing mood as it sent its waves crashing against the rugged shoreline. I heaved a sigh of relief that the fishermen were home for the weekend. It was mid January, and the serried rows of white-foamed breakers were accompanied by an occasional flurry of snowflakes. The streets were deserted, which was not unusual on such a night, especially as it was just after five o'clock in the evening. Being what was tradition-ally known as the "Lord's Day", Buckie had its usual "ghost-town" appearance. No doubt a few hardy souls would venture out to the various church services later in the evening. But I was glad of the solitude, for the curious observer may well have wondered why this solitary figure was heading towards the harbour on such a stormy night, with a "mysterious" bundle under his arm.

I shivered as I proceeded along the oldest part of the town, known as the Yardie, which virtually hugs the shore. It is composed of fishermen's cottages strung out in neat rows, each built with its gable facing the sea. This was obviously a very wise policy, and no doubt enabled the cottages to survive the ravages of many a storm. It meant, however, that the lanes separating the rows of cottages acted as a kind of wind tunnel when the wind was blowing in from the sea. Turning my collar up, I braced myself in preparation for the sudden gusts as I passed each lane.

As I passed the Yardie, I could faintly make out the silhouette of the North Church spire pointing starkly into the wintry sky. The salty tang of the sea was now given a distinct "fishy" flavour as the wind swept across the fish-curing yards which lined the approach to the harbour. Normally a veritable hive of activity, they were now wrapped in gloomy silence. Whilst not lending anything to the architectural beauty of the town, their economic importance more than compensated for their presence.

Leaving the shelter of their monotonous, nondescript walls, I bent my head to meet once again the full fury of the blast. I hoped no one had seen me as I turned towards the mouth of the harbour. When I reached the end of the pier I paused for a minute or two, the events that had led to my being there crowding into my mind. Slowly I raised my once treasured idols and with almost ritualistic solemnity, I threw them as far as I could into the dark waters. To my surprise, the parcel floated on the heaving surface for fully a minute, as if it were some kind of extension of my very being and didn't want to be severed from me. But slowly it sank beneath the heavy swell surging in from the open sea. They were gone. Only God knew the value I had placed on them in terms of prestige. But now I had buried these idols once and for all, not like Jacob under the oak tree, but under the foam-slicked billows of the Buckie harbour.

Shaking myself from my reverie, I quickly

turned and left the quay where the fishing boats heaved at their mooring ropes, as if impatient to get out once more to the freedom of the open sea. A personal battle had been fought and won. The contents of that parcel had symbolised my past life, and with that I was finished forever. A greater One now reigned supreme in my life. Pascal the French philosopher once said, "There is a God-shaped vacuum in every heart." The Lord had now taken up residence in mine, and there was no longer any room for the tinsel toys of this world. To express my love for Him in a public way, I was that very evening to follow Him through the waters of baptism, signifying on a spiritual plane, my death, burial and resurrection, with the One Who had given His all for me. The very thought of it drew from my lips another favourite hymn:

"O Christ in Thee my soul hath found,
And found in Thee alone,
The peace the joy I sought so long,
The bliss till now unknown.
Now none but Christ can satisfy,
None other name for me;
There's love, and life, and lasting joy
Lord Jesus found in Thee."

The wind tried to whip the words away, and the occasional wave thundering over the breakwater wall seemed determined to drown me out. Nevertheless I gave greater vent to a verse that had a deep significance for me:

"I tried the broken cisterns Lord,
But ah! the waters failed!
E'en as I stooped to drink they'd fled,
And mocked me as I wailed."

Leaving behin'd the fish-curing yards, I took the left turn up the steep hill to Cluny Square, on my way to the Gospel Hall where the baptism was to take place.

# Chapter 2

## ABANDONED

Along the Moray Firth coast the visitor can find many little villages and towns. Each could tell of days of great prosperity when the herring industry was at its height. Old photographs can still be proudly produced to show the various harbours crammed full of sailboats or drifters. Some old prints show literally thousands of barrels stacked along the quay. Some show the fishergirls hard at work gutting the fish. The prevailing impression presented by these scenes from the past is one of bustle and activity. Since a prosperous fishing industry, because of its very nature, supports a variety of other subsidiary industries, the tragedy is, that when it fails, so do the others. As a result, most of the harbours which shared in the great herring "bonanza", are now little more than havens for the pleasure-craft enthusiasts.

The town of Portsoy is a typical example. It once boasted, not only a progressive fishing industry, but also a prosperous merchant trade as well. It is located on a rugged shore-line between Banff, a few miles to the east, and Cullen, a few miles to the west. Before and after the Second World War, a casual visitor to the harbour would have been excused for thinking that it was the most derelict in the whole coast. Although they have since been modernised, at that time the harbour area was dominated by tall, gaunt, multi-storey warehouses, in an advanced state of disrepair. Some dated from the sixteenth century and gave a ghostly witness to more prosperous times. It was in a rented room, in a house located in the main thoroughfare of this town, that I was born on June 19th 1935. I was the third member of the family, and my mother was scarcely out of her teens. Within another year another one was added, and the four of us were boys. Within a few months after that my mother was expecting her fifth child.

I must, of course, depend on the information furnished by others, in order to describe the events of this period. There appears to be no doubt that the seeds of matrimonial disaster were sown then. To have four sons in as many years during a period of unprecedented economic hardship must have been a tremendous strain on a young mother, living in cramped accommodation. Sad to relate, smoking, drinking and gambling, all took their toll of a very meagre income. The moral standards of my father left much to be desired, and consequently the breakdown of the family was just a matter of time. It finally came when I was about two years of age.

Just prior to this domestic disaster, an incident took place which could well have led to my death, or, at the very least, my serious injury. The details were given to me by some of the people who had been present at the time. Apparently, when just a toddler and still unsteady on my feet, I somehow

managed to clamber up the stone slabs to the top
of the high parapet which shelters the Portsoy
harbour on the north side. Someone spotted me
gaily tottering along towards the highest point at
the mouth of the harbour. Occasional stumbles
did not deter me, and the screaming gulls wheeling
their reckless flight overhead, only added excitement to my exploit. At any point along the uneven
surface of the wall, a wrong step would have sent
me headlong on to the jagged rocks on the
seaward side of the parapet, or down on to the
stone slabs of the pier itself. A petrified group
gathered, but fear of the possible outcome para-
lysed them. My uncle happened to come on to the
scene and quickly summed up the situation.
Although partially lame since childhood, he quickly
clambered up to the top of the parapet and quietly
caught up with me. He swept me into his brawny
arms just as I had reached the end of the wall, to
the great relief of the spectators. He told me many
years later, that his biggest fear was that I would
spot him approaching and make a run for it. I had
the opportunity in recent times to walk along this
same parapet, and the full horror of what could
have happened really gripped me. Looking down
from the dizzy heights, I thought of the words of
David in the Old Testament: "There is but a step
between me and death". Needless to say, I lifted
up my heart to the God of Heaven in gratitude for
his preserving care over me as a child.

Attempts were made by my mother's parents in
Portsoy to salvage the marriage, but to no avail.
The whole affair must have been very distressing

to them both, but to my grandfather in particular. He was then a regular attender at the Salvation Army meetings in the town, and he was a highly respected member of the community. The news that the marriage had disintegrated reached my father's parents in Buckie in a rather dramatic form. It was heralded by a knock on their back door one afternoon. My grandmother, known to everyone in the neighbourhood as "Grannie", furnished me in later years with graphic details of what actually happened that day. As far as I was concerned, the incident was to affect the whole course of my life. Indeed it was to trigger off a whole series of events that were most assuredly to affect my eternal destiny.

"When I opened the door," Grannie explained, "all that I could see were four bairns looking up into my face. Your mother was running down the street, leaving her bairns behind." Grannie went on to describe how she ran after the fleeing figure of my mother, calling for her to come back to her children who were hysterical by this time. My mother ignored her appeals, and Grannie sadly retraced her steps to the pathetic group huddled on her doorstep. We were all shabbily dressed, and my youngest brother was less than a year old. She went on to describe the terrible plight she was faced with. She already had a grandson, a cousin of mine, under her care. He suffered from meningitis as a young child, and he required special attention. Now she was faced with the bleak prospect of having four more mouths to feed.

Long discussions were held between Grannie and some of my aunts who lived nearby. The social-welfare service, such as it was then, was contacted and advice sought. Placing us in the orphanage at Aberlour was at one point considered.

Further attempts were made to contact my mother. It was learned that my father, along with other fishermen, had left the area to make a better living at the trawling. Some went to Aberdeen, whilst others went to Fleetwood in England. It was in the latter that my father set up his permanent home. My mother had been left in Portsoy and she claimed that it was sheer desperation that forced her to abandon her children and follow him there to make some form of reconciliation. She had been left virtually destitute and, being so young, she was totally incapable of coping. Sanity was thrown to the wind and the result was four young, innocent children, left bewildered on a doorstep. She was carrying another baby and this was the only way that she could think of, to force my father to face up to his responsibilities. Sad to say, it is always the innocent who suffer in such "chess games" of matrimonial strife.

After some deliberation, my aunt, who lived next door, decided to take my youngest brother into her home to bring him up. Grannie decided to do the same for me. After some persuasion from various sources, my mother came north and took my other brothers away to Fleetwood. A reconciliation of some sort had taken place, and the marriage, if one could call it that, was re-established on a very shaky foundation.

Whilst all this is outside the range of my memory recall, I'm convinced it must have left psychological scars on my young mind. To be suddenly deprived of a mother's love at such a crucial stage of one's emotional development, must have a serious effect on one's personality in later life. One can indeed recall moments in early life, and, to a certain extent, in adult years, when one was almost overwhelmed by feelings of insecurity. There is no doubt in my own mind that such distressing feelings could well be traced back to the traumatic experience of parental rejection. If only parents would stop to think about the damage they do to their children when they selfishly treat their marriage vows with contempt, perhaps it would make them think again.

Perhaps traumatic experiences tend to sharpen the focus of one's memory at an earlier age than usual, but the next couple of years' events linger somewhere at the back of my mind. Different blurred images drift across the screen of my memory — scenes of anger; scenes of people, always talking, talking — a blurred and distorted kaleidescope of incidents. One such incident was the visit of my mother and father to Buckie. I was still under school age at the time. My brother and I were taken to Portsoy for the day. I can vividly recall waiting for the bus to take us back to Buckie. My parents had been drinking, and by this time they were in no state to be in charge of young children. At the bus-stop there was a bit of rowdiness, and a policeman came over from the police-station to find out what was going on. We were all brought into his office where my parents were questioned and admonished for their drunken behaviour, and for their irresponsibility with children.

In these days of so-called "broadmindedness", the liberal thinking public are no longer shocked to see a woman under the influence of drink in an open street. To be seen, however, in a quiet place like Portsoy at that time, with two young children at your side, was absolutely shocking. According to my brother, this is the earliest recollection that he has. This unpleasant experience must have made an indelible impression on his memory, for he was just about three years of age at that time. When my parents went away after this visit, I never saw them, or my other brothers, until seven years later. Our family was divided for good. There was no prospect of a healing of the breach.

# Chapter 3

## POVERTY

My grandfather had just retired from the sea. He had been a fisherman all his working life. There can be no doubt that the early part of his career was marked by prosperity. As a young man he had a share in a sailboat, and when he married, he brought his young bride to a new house in a district of Buckie, known as Buckpool. (His initials still adorn an engraved stone above the lintel of the front door.) How proud he must have been when he received the keys of his substantial new house. True, there was no proper sanitation apart from a dry latrine in an out-house. There was no electricity and the only running water came from an outside tap situated over a huge open drain. Every room was fitted with a gas-supply for lighting and there was a gas-tap at the side of the mantelshelf to which a gas-ring or gas-iron could be fitted. No doubt my grandfather fully intended to install all the latest facilities as they became available. But in the year 1895 these were few and far between. In any case he wasn't the type of person who would put himself in debt just to be "with it". Forty years later, however, when he decided to call it a day, not only were the amenities unchanged, but the house was a sad picture of neglect. He had long since given up his share of the boat. The house was no longer his in effect. Most of his working life had been marked by poverty, debt and despair. His latter working years had coincided with the Depression. Defeated, humiliated and embittered, he had good cause to think that "Fate" had dealt its last cruel blow.

In those days of economic slump every sector of industry was affected. As most fishermen along the Moray Firth coast were share-fishermen, they were particularly hard hit. At first they did not qualify for unemployment benefit because they were viewed as a special category of workers by the authorities. Humiliating means-tests were applied under the supervision of a group of local business men, who probed into the personal affairs of each claimant. This group had the power to decide whether or not any benefit should be awarded. One can imagine the degradation and consequent bitterness arising from such tests. When they finally managed to get benefit it was just a mere twenty-three shillings and sixpence per week for a married man with a family.

What was probably the most aggravating aspect of this unhappy period, was the desperate hopelessness of the situation. This led to despair in many cases, especially involving those with heavy family responsibilities. No matter how willing a man was to work in order to maintain his family, there always seemed to be some insurmountable problem to frustrate his efforts.

Whilst these problems were general, it is only fair to say that the fisherman had certain economic hazards peculiar to his occupation. For instance there were the terrible risks involved in the "settling up" system. This was a very complicated matter. After all expenses for a fishing trip were paid, e.g. for food, fuel and harbour dues, the balance of the gross earnings was divided equally into three portions. One portion went to the "ship", one went to the "nets" and the remainder went to the six or seven members of the crew. Only the stoker, the cook and the engineer had a fixed weekly wage. The portion that went to the share-members of the crew divided equally, the skipper getting exactly the same as the others. Those who owned part of the "fleet" of nets got an extra payment from the net portion. A man could have a half, a quarter, or even an eighth share of

A Buckie fishing boat

the "fleet", and was paid accordingly. From this money he had, however, to pay for the repair and renewal of his own nets. The more enterprising a fisherman was, the more he had to lose if things went wrong. If, as sometimes happened, the gross earnings were not sufficient to cover the expenses of the trip, the amount that was deficient was divided into the same three portions as was the balance when a trip had been prosperous. Apart from the men whose wages were assured, they had to "pay-in", often after several weeks of hard, back-breaking, heartbreaking toil. The owners of the nets had not only to pay in his quota for his labour share, but he had also to pay in the equivalent of his net share too. Similarly, the owner of the ship had to meet the "ship's share" of the deficit. So the irony of the whole thing was that these men were penalised for being the owners of the very gear, apart from which no fishing could have taken place at all. Needless to say, the unpredictable nature of the fishing industry at a time when there was no radar equipment to take the element of chance out of the search for fish, meant that the "settling up" system led to the ruin of many a keen fisherman.

As in every situation where the element of chance is predominant, there were no doubt those who became very wealthy, but for the most part the average fisherman had a very lean time of it. My grandfather, along with many a hardworking, honest man, had the bitter misfortune of being forced to incur debt to the grocer and the ship's chandler and so on, before the fishing season got underway, only to come home to his wife and family poorer and deeper in debt than when he left. One can only imagine the nervous strain and psychological pressures brought to bear on such seafaring families.

It should be put on record that a local family bakery, McWilliams by name, showed great consideration and kindness to many afflicted families in the town of Buckie. Their extreme, sacrificial generosity, made it clear to everyone that they put people before profits. For a mere pittance, a poor family could get a substantial supply of bread to tide them over. The members of this family were committed Roman Catholics, and their attitude, plus the unstinting praise of the community, was quite remarkable in a day when there was very little religious tolerance.

There seems to be little doubt that the First World War dealt a crippling blow to the fishing industry. Prior to the war there had been a period of abounding prosperity. Large fleets of herring boats just couldn't cope with the enormous demand for supplies of salt herrings from countries such as Germany and Russia. The Scottish fishing industry was geared to meet the boom trade, and everything looked well for the future. The war put an end to all their aspirations, and from that economic disaster it has never really recovered.

What about Grannie, who had no doubt to carry the heaviest burden of the grinding poverty? She was born in 1877 in a small district of Buckie known as Portessie. At fifteen she was travelling to places such as Lerwick and Great Yarmouth, working at the "gutting". The gutting of fish was a messy, cold, and very poorly paid job, but the North-East girls possessed a spirit of buoyancy and love of fun that helped them turn such drudgery into something almost enjoyable. Working for long hours in all kinds of weather, in draughty open yards, did not dampen their spirits. They took great pride in their work, and most of them could gut the fish at lightning speed. They could gut and grade, that is, select the fish according to size, sixty to seventy herrings a minute. A barrel could hold up to one thousand herrings and three barrels were skilfully packed each hour, gutters and packers working in teams.

Although the girls tied cloth strips around each finger for protection, the sharp knife sometimes cut their fingers as they worked at high speed. The salt would cause excruciating pain to the unfortunate victims, and medical help, an expensive matter in those days, was sometimes required if poison set in. Of course there was no such thing as compensation in those early days.

Weekends were happy occasions. Scottish fishermen did not fish on a Sunday as a rule, (things have changed a lot since then). It was a time of reunion when fathers, brothers and lovers met to discuss the events of the week, and to talk of home and future plans. Invariably there was a time of hymn-singing when favourites would be sung from the popular hymn book *Sacred Songs and Solos*, compiled by Sankey. Nearly everyone went to a place of worship, and open-air services were a great feature in Great Yarmouth. In Lerwick, the menfolk were invited to the huts where the girls lived, to enjoy some home-baking. The harshness of the week's work seemed to intensify the sheer delight of such light-hearted occasions. No doubt being away from the more restricted environment of home, allowed many a romance to blossom.

Grannie was not a Christian. She paid lip service to the Church of Scotland, but she knew very little about God's plan of salvation. She had attended Sunday School and could recite several long passages from the Bible. Several religious "Revivals" had taken place during her early childhood, but it was my impression that she treated them with suspicion, if not with scorn. Going to church, however, was the thing everyone was expected to do, and so she went along with the rest.

When she got married her gutting days were over, and she settled down to the role of housewife. With a large family to raise and a husband at sea, her days were filled with the endless task of knitting, washing and mending nets. A fisherman's wife was expected at that time to support, at a distance, the trade by which the family survived. As fortune was smiling on them at that time, Grannie did not seem to mind the drudgery too much.

As prosperity gave way to poverty, and poverty to debt, and debt to despair, it was Grannie who arranged for the house to be mortgaged. In sheer desperation she handed over the title deeds to some estate agent in exchange for a certain sum of money, to be repaid with interest over a period of time. This mortgage was to hang over their heads like a heavy cloud for the rest of their married life. On a few occasions, it became the sole cause of the rare but bitter arguments that blighted their happiness as husband and wife.

To augment my grandfather's meagre and uncertain income, Grannie went out to mend nets for other people. This work was poorly paid, but she was grateful for the extra money. Of course better days were always hoped for, but alas they never came. From as far afield as Fraserburgh, whole lorry-loads of nets came to be mended in Grannie's loft. This ensured work all the year round. During the cold winter months the nets were taken down from the loft to the living room, where they could be mended whilst Grannie enjoyed the heat from the hob-range fire. To the houseproud housewife this would have been a nightmarish arrangement, for the nets were by no means clean, and the room was soon filled with dust and clippings. To Grannie there was no other alternative, for life was now for her a vicious circle of work and debt. This was my new home.

# Chapter 4

## SUPERSTITION

Not surprisingly, I was extremely nervous as a young child. I seemed to possess an over-active imagination. As I lay in bed at night I would imagine all sorts of things. I would imagine that someone else was in the bed, for I could hear them breathing beside me. I would stare at the old-fashioned wallpaper and the design would appear to form weird shapes which terrified me. There was a piece of furniture which had scrolls carved on either side, and the wood had a veneer finish. Although the veneer assumed horrible faces, it was the carvings that really frightened me. To my young mind they seemed to look straight at me with malevolent anger. I was rapidly becoming a nervous-wreck.

Things got so bad that I just could not sleep on my own. When my cousin came home from the sea it was all right, but when I was left on my own I went from bad to worse. I would try to fall asleep, usually with my head under the bedclothes, but invariably I would reach a climax of fear and start screaming. The sweat would simply pour off my body and I would shake uncontrollably. Eventually I would be taken through to my grandparents' room and allowed to sleep at the bottom of their bed. My grandfather was very patient with me and he was often a real source of comfort. For a while I was allowed to sleep with them without having to endure the terrifying nightly ritual. No doubt they were getting fed up with my carry-on in any case, and didn't want to be disturbed every night. Sometimes my grandfather went to bed a little earlier than usual because he suffered from bronchial trouble. For me it was sheer bliss to listen to his stories of the sea. Never did he mention his disappointments. He always talked about the good times and I just lay there and followed him in flights of fantasy on his voyages of adventure. His knowledge of poetry was considerable, considering he was a relatively uneducated man who had left school at the age of twelve. In fact he made up poems of his own which I can remember to this day.

I have no doubt that I could have adjusted myself to my new environment without too much trouble. The unaccountable fears and feelings of insecurity would probably have disappeared with the help of my grandparents' understanding, had it not been for another quirk of fate. An uncle of mine, without doubt the favourite of my grandparents, was tragically killed when his ship was blown up by an enemy mine in the English Channel. They were overcome with grief. Things were never the same in my new home. Prior to the tragedy, Christmas was celebrated in the usual way, with decorations and a bit of merriment. For once in the year this dark, drab home was brightened with a bit of glitter, and the laughter hid the poverty. No decorations were ever put up after my uncle's death. The last vestige of happiness seemed to drain away after this, and for me there seemed to be an atmosphere of perpetual mourning.

Even my grandfather seemed to lose heart altogether. Something had died within him and I knew that I could no longer expect his attention as once I could. The loneliness, the insecurity, and all the hidden fears, emerged to the surface of my personality and gripped me with greater intensity. A new emotion was now making its presence felt — the emotion of bitterness. Instead of running away I was prepared to fight these cruel phantoms that had plagued my life. A smouldering resentment began to eat away at my very inwards. This was occasionally fanned into a blaze of fury and often found full expression in some form of aggressive behaviour. On one particular occasion, I remember retaliating with a knife when my cousin taunted me with something which has long gone from my memory. Had others not intervened in time, one shudders to think of what may have happened.

Our home became a breeding ground for bitterness, and for another specific reason. A family who lived across the street professed to be Christians. Indeed they were fine people and were ardent church members. Because he was a Christian, one member of the family felt he could not take part in any form of combat. He felt it was his duty, as a Christian, to abstain from taking life. He was allowed to work in a local shipyard, since such work was considered to be of national importance. This was frowned upon by my grandparents, whose sons were taking active part in the war effort. When news of my uncle's death came, the initial grief was soon changed to implacable venom against this family across the street. Filth of every description was continually hurled across the street under cover of night. White feathers and emotive clippings from newspapers, found their way through their letterbox. We were plagued with rats at this time, and when any were caught or poisoned, they were surreptitiously tied to the handle of their door. Many other schemes of a diabolical nature were thought up, but one is too ashamed to relate them in detail. As a young boy I got involved in quite a number of the escapades. I quite enjoyed what I considered to be great fun, although I did not realise at the time the real motives behind such activity. The poor people, who had shown such tremendous tolerance, reached a point when they just couldn't take any more. They were forced to bring in the police, and as a result, Grannie was taken to court. This only infuriated Grannie even more, and the bitterness was intensified. It was impossible for me to be in the midst of this hostile environment and not be tainted by it. The conversation was always about the religious "hypocrites" across the street. Looking back, I think it affected me in two ways. Firstly, it taught me that hatred and violence were the norm, and secondly, that anything associated with Christianity was hypocritical and had to be opposed. Although the court case put an end to our despicable behaviour, the hatred smouldered on for years, with occasional outbursts.

News came that my father's ship had been sunk by enemy action. A German submarine had surfaced near their converted trawler and they were ordered into the small boats. They were allowed to leave the immediate vicinity before a few shells sank their vessel Of the two small boats, only one reached the safety of land. My father happened to be on this one and they were rescued at Tobermory. Whilst they hadn't the same esteem for my father as for their late son, my grandparents allowed this near-tragedy to stir up fresh animosity against our neighbours.

I don't know if Grannie had always been superstitious, but I do know that she certainly manifested a very superstitious side of her personality during this period. I suppose most people are, to a certain extent, superstitious. Even in a so-called highly civilised society like our own, we come across many people who "touch wood", or avoid number thirteen. In a fishing community, where there is a strong element of danger involved in one's livelihood, and where the elements play an important part, such superstitions can be an extremely important factor. Although, as stated, the modern fish-finding equipment has almost ruled out the element of chance in the process of fishing, old established superstitions will emerge from time to time. In times of great stress such as a wartime situation, or when a fishing vessel is lost, the old superstitions lurking beneath the surface sometimes come to the forefront. To avoid misfortune, old established superstitious customs are occasionally revived.

Lucky charms and taboos become more meaningful
to those who feel there are opposing forces too
powerful for them to cope with. I would say that
Grannie came into this category. Quite apart
from the heartache caused by the war she had lost
faith in the idea of a benevolent God, and I'm sure
she felt that she had to look elsewhere for the
answers to her problems. She certainly placed a
great deal of stress on the importance of
premonitions, dreams and visions. "If you dream
about the dead you will hear something about the
living," was one of her sayings. She was always
making some reference to something she had
dreamt the previous night.

The night she got a "visit" from my late uncle,
prior to his death, was a favourite story. Every
time we had a visitor the same story was told. The
story was always preceded by Grannie taking
down my uncle's photograph from the mantelshelf
and giving it a wipe. There would be a time of
weeping and then she would proceed with the
story. It went something like this: One night she
was awakened from her sleep with the strange
feeling that someone was wanting to speak to her.
Looking about the room which was lit by a
paraffin lamp, she could make out a shadowy
figure drawing near to her bed. Almost
immediately she recognised the figure to be that
of her son. After a slight pause he spoke to her in a
quiet normal voice and passed on a cryptic
message, "There was never a second without a
third." The form gradually disappeared into thin
air. The next day the news was brought that he

had been killed. Grannie had her own interpretation of the strange message. Apparently
two young men from our neighbourhood, both
friends of my late uncle, had been killed in the
war. She firmly believed that she was being told
personally by her son that he was going to be next.
You can imagine that this sort of conversation
didn't help my nervous disposition. What was
probably no more than a hallucination, the
product of anxiety over a favourite son, was
nevertheless made very real to me after hearing
about it so often.

I can recall another incident that took place not
long after Grannie had her "vision". We had a
visitor from Glasgow staying with us at the time.
Grannie had just related her usual story and was,
as can be expected, quite upset.

"Would you like to speak to Johnnie?" our
visitor asked a rather startled Grannie. Indeed
Grannie couldn't answer her for a moment or two
because the question had been so unexpected, and
had taken her completely by surprise. She
certainly wasn't at all sure what was meant by the
question. I sat on the metal fender at the front of
the fire, totally mystified by the strange
conversation that followed. The visitor assured
Grannie that there was nothing to be afraid of,
but she wasn't too keen about it. This was an area
of superstition, beyond her experience, and I
think she was genuinely afraid. She finally
consented however, and the gas-mantel was
turned down low. The only people in the room
were, Grannie, the visitor, two aunts and myself.

In the semi-darkness, the face of the visitor assumed a strange mask-like appearance as she slowly swayed from side to side in a trance. She seemed to my young mind to be speaking to unseen "individuals" and yet gave a form of commentary to my relatives now and then. I could hear her calling my late uncle's name, and her comments to Grannie indicated that he was coming in a little while. She was warning her to be ready to speak to him, and I could see Grannie clenching and relaxing her fists nervously. The tension mounted as the visitor's voice became louder and louder.

"He's coming! He's coming!" The pitch of her voice sent a chill down my spine. One of my aunts started to weep quietly. When the visitor spoke, again she burst out into uncontrollable sobs.

"He's here!"

The words had scarcely left the visitor's mouth when, without warning, three very loud knocks were hammered on the back door. Although they occurred at a moment of extreme tension, I had never heard such loud knocks on our door before. I sat riveted to my front-seat perch, unable to take in what was happening. The fear shown by my aunt and the nervousness of Grannie were transmitted to me, so I just buried my head in my hands, waiting for something to happen.

"We'll have no more of this!" Grannie's voice was firm with a tinge of anger. Reaching up to turn up the gas in the mantel she told the visitor to stop right away. The spell was broken. Nothing more was said about the unearthly knocks on the

door. The subject was changed and never raised
in my hearing for many years.

When the matter was discussed with Grannie
later in life, I discovered that my youthful
impressions had not been coloured by my
imagination. It was exactly as I had remembered
it. To my aunts and Grannie it had been a very
weird and emotional experience indeed. She also
told me that when she was out mending nets the
day after the strange incident, she happened to
mention it to her fellow workers. She was taken
aback by the unexpected response of one of them.
She had expressed her disappointment that she
hadn't been present, for she had been engaged in
similar activities herself for some time. One can
safely assume that such practices have been more
widespread than was realised. A war situation,
with many loved ones being suddenly killed, no
doubt brings it out into the open.

To the outsider, the importance of superstition
to a person like Grannie, borders on the ludicrous.
But we must remember that her cultural roots
were firmly embedded in a system of beliefs that
had been handed down from generation to
generation. A lot of research has been done
concerning the folk-lore of the fishing communities. From such, emerges the recurring
theme of the strange beast referred to as the
"Cockie Coo" by the fisherfolk of Buckie, in the
not-so-distant past. From what I learned from my
grandfather, this belief was very strong in the
area at one time. There seems to be no doubt that
this beast in the form of a cow, was Satan. It was

believed that this strange beast roamed about the area ready to seize the unwary. My grandfather claimed that he had seen this animal himself when he was a young boy. He had been in the process of stealing hooks from fishing lines that had been stretched along the beach. It was late one summer's evening and there was no one about. Glancing up, he was astonished to see this big cow-like animal coming along the stones of the beach. The odd thing was that there was no sound whatsoever as the animal walked along the loose gravel. He fled as fast as his young legs could carry him, and he didn't stop until he was safely inside the house. Years afterwards I considered this to be Buckie's version of "Wee Wullie Winkie" and dismissed it as having been my grandfather's way of getting me in at a decent hour at night, or to refrain from stealing. Although he told the story on several occasions, I was sure he had his tongue in his cheek each time. I was surprised to hear, however, a strikingly similar story about a similar animal in another part of the coast many years later. All the details, even the silent walk of the animal, were almost identical. Perhaps my grandfather was perfectly sincere after all. Perhaps this legendary-animal story, no doubt a carry-over from dark superstitious ages, was so deeply entrenched in his subconscious mind that his feelings of guilt, as he stole the hooks, projected this fearsome "animal" before his eyes.

The sea itself played such an important role in the lives of the fisherfolk that it assumed a power to be feared. To them it was a living, animated "being", capable of different moods. The sea gave or withheld the fish according to the mood it happened to be in. They believed that the sea could be offended or placated just like any other living being. For example, to pick up a body at sea was considered at one time to be tantamount to robbing it of its rightful prey, and was sure to raise its anger. A body washed up on shore was consequently buried as near to the shoreline as possible.

The desire to avert all sorts of calamities and misfortune at sea led to the development of many odd habits. To be asked where he was going was enough to turn a Buckie fisherman on his heels and not go to sea that day, for such a question he believed, would have brought bad luck. If he met a minister, or an "ill-fitted" person, as he made for the harbour, he looked upon such an encounter as a sure harbinger of bad luck. He would either go home and not go to the sea that day, or indulge in a variety of means of breaking the bad luck, such as spitting or touching "cauld iron" as soon as possible.

Certain animals such as rabbits and pigs were never to be mentioned on board a fishing boat. They could, of course, be referred to in an indirect way. The word "salmon" was strictly taboo, as were certain surnames such as Ross and Coull, which ended in a double consonant. Whistling, especially on board a boat, was severely frowned upon. It was believed that the wind could be raised by whistling and anyone, who did so, ran a serious risk of being accused of deliberately inviting trouble.

The Banffshire coast appears to have been a favourite haunt for devil-worshippers and those involved in witchcraft. Each community has its own oral tradition of black and white magic. According to tradition, the Bin Hill, which stands as an ageless sentinel behind Buckie, was once a favourite venue for witches'covens. How reliable these stories are, is of course another matter. But there is no question about the fact that fisherfolk were, and still are to a certain extent, very superstitious. And as for Grannie, there was woven into the very warp and woof of her attitude to human existence, a very strong superstitious element. Her attitude no doubt coloured my own thinking. Certainly I found myself asking such questions as "Why am I here? Where am I going after death? Has life any meaning at all?"and so on. I never found any answers and I gradually came to the conclusion that there were no answers. I was just a piece of flotsam, floating on the sea of life and being carried by the current of nameless, impersonal forces, too big and powerful for me to resist. I was sharing Grannie's fatalistic view of existence.

# Chapter 5

## TARZIE

What had caused the plague of rats already referred to may provide an amusing diversion from the general gloom of my story thus far. These undesirable creatures were attracted by the sensational arrival of a not too-hygienic character called "Tarzie". As his name suggests, he was a monkey, and had he been able to speak, what an interesting story he could have told us. The poor fellow had been a victim of Hitler's cruel war machine. As many eye witnesses can testify, in the midst of the confusion of Dunkirk's battlescarred beaches, all types of animals could be seen running about in sheer panic. Racehorses screamed in fear as the German planes strafed the retreating forces. As the guns roared and the bombs exploded, dogs could be seen darting around, craven with fear. A little monkey was spotted, ambling around like a little old man, dragging a broken arm. The pathetic creature melted the heart of a passing soldier who lifted him up ever so gently and helped him to take part in what was probably the greatest evacuation in history. Another kind soul put his arm in splints and cared for him until he had recovered. Shortly afterwards he was given to my father, and he in turn arranged for him to be brought to Buckie. In this roundabout way he found himself a refugee in our home, and he was given his name, which was very soon to be on every youngster's lips, at least in the Buckpool section of the town.    It isn't too difficult to imagine the stir that our new lodger caused. It was more than likely that Tarzie was the first real monkey that most of the young people of Buckie had ever seen, so they were all very excited about it. Scarcely a day passed without a group of youngsters gathering in the backyard to observe his antics. I've no doubt that some made a daily pilgrimage to our mini zoo, for there was very little to do at that time in a place like Buckie. I can remember feeling very important because we were the owners of Tarzie, and the topic of conversation at school always came round to his latest exploits.

In spite of his very appreciative daily audience, he sometimes became discontented and made a daring break for freedom. (Almost forty years afterwards I still meet people who remember those daring escapes of Tarzie with the greatest affection.) Normally he had a kind of harness around his waist to which was clipped a fairly lengthy, but light, link-chain. This was fastened in turn to the doorpost of the shed where he was housed. Sometimes, however, this cunning character managed to unclip the chain and scamper over the rooftops. When this happened, literally hundreds of youngsters appeared as if from nowhere, thronging the street to watch every move of the cheeky culprit. The more excited the children were, the more daring he became. He would screech defiance at his would-be captors, to the immense pleasure of his hundreds of young fans who were definitely on his side. On one such memorable occasion he had been chased into a neighbour's garden where there was an apple tree, simply laden with beautiful apples. The owner was very proud, and rightly so, of his tidy garden, and especially of his apple tree. Imagine his vehement anger as our scurrilous scamp ventured into his leafy sanctuary. But worse was to follow. Hundreds of children, totally oblivious of his foaming threats, thronged into the garden after Tarzie, who by then had been attracted to the tree. When the owner realised that his threats were being ignored, and his lovely garden being destroyed, he almost went berserk. He waved his arms and shouted to no avail. He was still ignored by all, that is all apart from Tarzie himself. He seemed to spot the owner right away from his vantage point and he wasn't too happy with the intrusion. To show his disapproval he started to pelt the owner with the apples. It could well have been the case that the apples were intended for anyone who happened to attract his attention, but certainly the bulk of them were flying in the direction of the hapless owner, who had by this time turned his venom on the cause of the uproar. But Tarzie had had enough. With a deft swing on a high branch he soared through the air and landed on a nearby wash-house, pausing to give his audience another cheeky screech before setting off again on his wild career. Without fail, he turned up as usual at a late hour, looking about his shed for something to eat.

A little coat was made for Tarzie and it was funny to see him dressed up to keep out the cold. When it was very frosty he was taken into the living-room to keep warm beside the fire. It was very amusing to see him heating his little black hands on the stainless-steel ornamental ball that projected from the side of the hob-grate. On the metal fender were engraved the words "Home Sweet Home" and Tarzie certainly made himself at home. But as one can easily gather by now, it certainly wasn't the cleanest of homes.

This privilege was hastily withdrawn after he had inadvertently been left in the house by himself. Finding himself alone, he apparently had started to investigate the inner secrets of the cabinets in the room. He found shiny ornaments which, when dropped on to the linoleum floor, made funny tinkling noises. He didn't stop until he had covered the whole floor with a multi-coloured shower of glazed confetti. The ornaments were Grannie's best china, her prized wedding-gifts and presents brought from Great Yarmouth when times were more prosperous. Grannie, not surprisingly, took this very badly, since they were her only surviving link with those happier days. She never forgave Tarzie, and had little time for him after that.

We had neither the facilities nor the expertise to care for such an animal properly. I was too young to really understand what was necessary for his well-being, and my grandparents were too old to cope. As a result the shed soon became absolutely filthy. In the summer the stench was simply overpowering. The poor creature's health began to suffer. During the night we sometimes heard him screeching and we wondered what was causing the commotion. Then we spotted the sores on his tail. It suddenly dawned upon us that he was being attacked by rats during the night. His tail became a terrible mess of putrid sores and his general health rapidly deteriorated. It was indeed a sad morning when Tarzie was found dead. We buried him beneath the lilac tree in our tiny garden amidst scenes of genuine mourning. Tarzie had brought a bright beam into the dark years of war for many youngsters. He diverted their attention away from the harsh realities of the hostilities that took many of their fathers away from home to face danger and death. Some children had suffered the loss of a father and Tarzie's coming on to the scene acted as a healing balm to many of them. I look back now with sadness because I'm sure he died through neglect. Were such a thing to happen today, the R.S.P.C.A. would certainly have something to say.

Poison was set to get rid of the rats which were obviously increasing in number. Several were found dead each day. By the end of the week almost twenty had been poisoned. As stated, these horrible creatures were used to further the cause of the feud that still was in full swing at this time.

# Chapter 6

## EARLY IMPRESSIONS

I don't know if Tarzie's demise had anything to do with it, but about this time I became fascinated with the finality of death. Death was something quite common in our neighbourhood. With the railway-line just a few hundred yards away, there were regular fatalities among the many dogs and cats of the area. The gory dismembered carcass usually drew an audience from our youthful ranks. I had a wide range of pets myself, and I often tried to rescue any injured wild birds, such as seagulls and jackdaws. Nearly every one of them died, so I was no stranger to death. Furthermore, there was a slaughterhouse not far away, and this was a Mecca for the less squeamish young lads of the vicinity. During the summer holidays we would gather at the railway-station to watch the cattle being unloaded. The sheep arrived in big lorries. At the slaughterhouse we would watch the sheep and cows being killed. This seemed to give my companions a weird sense of pleasure, but secretly the whole procedure filled me with unspeakable horror. I thought there was something repugnant about the way they dragged the animals to their death. Inwardly I wanted to cry out in defence of those helpless, dumb animals who struggled so much to avoid their tormentors. I knew my friends would think I was soft if I even expressed my inner feelings, so I pretended to enjoy the spectacle as well. After all, only the toughest of us could watch the massacre without flinching. This was no place for the soft or squeamish, and I wanted to be considered as one of the toughest members of our neighbourhood. It gave us some kind of prestige and standing in the sight of our peers. So I watched. The strong healthy animal would be dragged in, foaming at the mouth and eyes rolling with fear. A bolt was fired into its skull from the barrel of a special gun. The crumpled heap fell to the floor. A long piece of wire was pushed through the hole in the animal's skull and down its spinal column. This made the ungainly mass jerk in the most grotesque fashion in all directions. The carcase was then hoisted up off the floor by pulleys, and within a few minutes the animal was reduced to steaming, quivering sides of meat, and slung up on hooks.

I would often ponder why such heartless killing was necessary. "These animals have no choice in the matter," I used to tell myself. Death was so final and the very finality began to disturb me. "But why should there be death at all?" I kept asking myself. Baffled by such immense questions I could only resort to the only answer my young mind had — I was just like the sheep and cows, at the mercy of impersonal forces. Whatever these forces were I hated them for their heartless cruelty, but I knew I could do nothing about it.

I remember well the first human corpse I saw.

A cousin of about four years of age was knocked down and killed by a bus. His body was placed in a little white coffin, trimmed here and there with silver. I can remember gazing in blank amazement at the familiar, yet lifeless face. He looked just like a sleeping doll. "Was this really him? Why was he lying there in that box? Why wasn't he playing on the beach nearby? Would I never see him alive again? Why doesn't someone make him better? Why? Why? Why?" A thousand questions raced through my young mind. I stood there nonplussed, a cauldron of emotions beginning to well-up within my bosom. The mystery and the finality of death was too much for my young mind to take in. The experience had a profound effect upon me, and even today the sight of silver ornaments brings to mind the day when I peered into that coffin.

During my early youth I can recall at least one fleeting, favourable impression of a religious nature. A small group of Salvation Army members regularly conducted open-air services in various streets of the town. Sometimes one would give his testimony or preach a short Gospel Message. Some would play their concertinas whilst others would keep time with their tambourines. They were certainly bright and breezy services in keeping with the Army tradition.

I shall never forget a delighful, rather tubby character, known affectionately in the town as "Blin' Jimmie". I can visualise in my mind one particularly beautiful summer's evening. The setting sun cast a fiery brand across the Moray Firth, and almost seemed reluctant to go down below the Caithness hills. This good man, with his face radiant with an inner joy and his sightless eyes turned Heavenwards, sang from his heart as he played his concertina, "There is sunshine in my soul today, more glorious and bright, than shines in any earthly sky, for Jesus is my light."

"He's blind," I reflected. "He can't see that beautiful sunset that has turned the sky above Lossiemouth into a blaze of fire. Yet he sings of a sunshine in his soul. What can he be singing about? What does he mean? How can Jesus be his Light?"

I surveyed the group huddled together at the top of the brae. The service was over and the silence of the evening was now intensified. The only sounds to be heard were the plaintive cry of a gull homeward bound, and the gentle swish of a truant wave caressing the shore. Had anyone spoken to me about eternal matters during those few fleeting moments I would have listened. But the little group had now dispersed, the sun had set and the slightest hint of a cool breeze was wafting in from the Moray Firth.

This was the cue for the spiritual portcullis of my soul to come down with a shudder. "This religious business is not for the likes of me," I concluded. It was all right for Blin' Jimmie and such like. Obviously his religion had helped him to overcome his physical handicap and had given some kind of meaning to what I considered to be a very restricted existence. I realised that the old, the handicapped, the mentally weak and so on, all needed some kind of psychological crutch to lean upon. In their weakness they could look to religion to provide them with such a crutch. They could imagine that there was some kind of power, greater than their own, made available to them if they took an interest in religious matters. Faced with life's cruel disappointments, they could draw comfort and consolation from such an illusion. The thought of some Heavenly Utopia, where the sorrows of life would be past, was sufficient to tide them through life. This prospect had brought the glow to Jimmie's face. I was now sure of that. In a condescending way I felt sorry for such people, but I would have been the last to try to dispel such illusions. No, it would be a shame to do that. Whilst not verbalised in that way, these were my feelings as I pondered over the little incident that had impressed me, albeit momentarily. But now I was convinced that all religious matters were entirely foreign to my personal philosophy, so off with my chums I ran, shouting at the uniformed figures melting into the distance, "Salvation Army frees from sin, takes you to Heaven in a carbine tin."

On several occasions I went with some of my chums to a "Magic Lantern" meeting. I cannot remember any of the pictures that were shown, or any of the comments made by those conducting the meetings. We really only went there for the promised cup of tea, and the possibility of getting a laugh at someone else's expense. Whoever was in charge must have found us more than a handful, for they were totally incapable of controlling us, or preventing our mischievous intentions from being carried out. I can remember one girl in the audience hurling abuse at us. Jean, as she was called, suffered from a glandular disorder and was, as a result, very stout. Of course we encouraged the banter and soon the poor girl was livid with rage and the audience was convulsed with laughter. Any spiritual effect on the youngsters gathered, was completely destroyed by our presence, and I'm sure the organisers must have heaved a sigh of relief when we sought our amusement elsewhere.

From the upper Buckpool area of Buckie where I lived, one had a panoramic view of the Moray Firth. Ten miles across the bay the town of Lossiemouth dominated the skyline. During the war there was constant activity in the Firth. Aeroplanes continually flew in and out from the Lossiemouth aerodrome. Occasional submarines, destroyers, and aircraft-carriers, made their presence known in the area. There was always someone on hand with a pair of powerful binoculars to give us a close-up view of the various ships.

On the 26th October 1940, three German Heinkel III bombers attacked the airbase at Lossiemouth. I can remember standing in the crowd at the top of the brae and looking across the water towards Lossiemouth. The unusual drone of the German planes, and the sound of the bombs exploding, stand out vividly in my memory. It was all so exciting to me, for as yet I hadn't appreciated the full horrors of war. Apparently one German plane was destroyed, but as it crashed, it demolished a house, containing, ironically, a family that had left the London area to escape the blitz. I'm led to believe that the whole family was wiped out.

Such large-scale activity brought the inevitable disasters in its wake. Many planes ended up in the sea, several of them piloted by young trainees. A motor-torpedo boat ran aground near the harbour at Buckie, and scores of souvenir hunters converged on the scene of the wreck. Sometimes interesting debris was washed up on to the beach, so a watchful eye was kept, especially after a storm. There was the constant danger of a mine being washed on to the rocks, but we were well warned about the dangers at home and at school.

One day a shattering explosion made my chums and I jerk upright and look towards Portgordon, a village about a mile from Buckpool. Shortly afterwards someone brought the tragic news. Three boys had been searching for fragments from a large German sea-mine which had been washed ashore and eventually blown up by the bomb disposal squad. In their search the boys had entered a nearby minefield. A mine exploded and one boy was killed instantly. Another died one hour later, whilst a third miraculously escaped with bruising, having been shielded from the blast by his friends. Horrific, gory accounts of the tragedy filtered around the district, and filled us with a sense of awe for a while. As I sat on the wooden fence, I watched the funeral procession ascending the brae. I don't know what I had expected to see, but after the grim stories, I was surprised to see two ordinary coffins, side by side in the same hearse. I have a vivid impression of the sun glinting off the varnish of the coffins as the procession reached the brow of the hill, and headed towards the place of interment.

Three potential spies, two men and a woman, were landed near Portgordon from a sea-plane one night. Their plans had to be changed when their bicycles were lost from their dinghy as they came ashore. One man and the woman were arrested at the Portgordon railway station. The other man walked to Buckie to catch the train to Edinburgh and was eventually arrested at Waverley station. The two men were subsequently executed but the woman's life was spared. To a young child this was all very exciting.

# Chapter 7

## YOUTHFUL PLOYS

Later on in the war another airbase was constructed about three miles west of Buckie. The workmen came from all parts of the country and were accommodated in private homes in the area. We had two men staying with us and I have often wondered since, what they thought of their primitive surroundings. Both of them came from Lesmahagow, and they must have been happy enough for they both corresponded with Grannie for many years after the war. All the men were picked up and transported by trucks each morning and taken home at night. Each evening we waited for the yellow trucks to come in sight. As soon as we saw them in the distance, we ran down the brae to meet them at the sharp bend where they had to slow down. This gave us the chance to leap on to the tailboard and get a lift to the top, where we immediately ran down to repeat the process.

It can be seen by now that the brae, or "Back Brae" as it was called, was the very hub of our activities. Winter or summer it was the favourite rendezvous of all the young people. At the bottom there was a trough for watering the horses which were in common use at that time. At this spot they were rested and watered before making the steep ascent with their heavy loads. We didn't worry too much about the poor horse as we darted on to the back-axle to get a lift to the top. The poor creature, with foam spewing from its mouth, had to carry the extra weight of about half a dozen boys up a very steep hill. Sometimes the driver lashed his whip at us, but he soon gave up when he saw how determined we were.

Needless to say the making of "cairties" was a favourite pastime. These were made from a small plank of wood, an old fish-box, and four pram wheels. These were steered with great dexterity and at high speed down our favourite brae. (Such ploys are out of the question nowadays because of the volume of traffic.)

Buckpool is, like the rest of this coastal belt, a raised beach. The grassy banks are a feature of the area. At the lower part of the raised beach the railway threaded its way along the coast. We were on the Aberdeen to Elgin route, and trains passed at regular intervals every day except Sunday. In fact the arrival of the train acted as a time signal for us, in days when watches were non-existent as far as we were concerned. A common pastime associated with the trains was the placing of coins and nails on to the metal rails. It was our hope that a half-penny could be flattened to the size of a penny, and be passed as such over the counter of the sweetie shop. Nails were flattened to make improvised knife blades. To know if there was a train due to come, we lay down on to the track and put our ear to the line. The vibrations could be felt even when the train was several miles away. Sometimes the grassy banks were set alight from the sparks which belched from the train's funnel. Far from putting out the fires, we took the opportunity to spread them until the whole area was covered with a heavy pall of smoke.

Although I enjoyed most, if not all of those simple ploys, my special interest was the fishing for edible crabs (called partans) and lobsters. In fact most of my spare time was spent among the rocks armed with a "cleek", searching every likely rock cleft. One soon developed a good knowledge of the best areas. Older, more experienced fishermen were carefully followed, and mental notes were made of their successful haunts for future reference. The claws of the partans were tied together, and they were carried home in triumph as bubbles frothed from them. Any lobsters caught had to be boiled alive, so little time was wasted in getting them into the pot. Oddly enough, my concern for the fate of living creatures did not extend to these crustaceans.

In days when there were no television sets and Community Centres, the young people had to invent their own means of enjoyment. During the dark winter evenings, the game of "follow-the-leader" was the one I enjoyed most. This involved following the most daring member of the group as he led us through private gardens, over fences, along dykes, over the roofs of sheds and down pipes and so on. We would find ourselves at the other end of the town after having travelled across literally dozens of private gardens and out of the way premises. Being small of build and very agile, this type of escapade appealed to me. The more risk involved the better I enjoyed it. I was always prepared to take up a challenge and my sense of adventure was very keen. Many a time a furious householder spotted us and chased us, brandishing a broom or similar weapon. This sent the adrenalin racing through our veins and intensified the fun of the evening.

Both my brother and I worked as milkboys whilst still at primary school. This consisted of working with a milkroundsman at the weekends to begin with. Later on we were initiated as fully-fledged barrowboys. In a place like Buckie with a very scattered milkround, it was more convenient to have the main round with the horse and cart, with a few subsidiary little barrow rounds serving the out of way streets and lanes. Several crates of milk were deposited at certain strategic points along the delivery route. These were collected by the barrowboys and distributed, each working in his own allocated district. My brother and I worked together for several years at this type of work.

My brother was more fortunate than I in his place of abode. He lived in a recently-built council house which had all the mod. cons. He was certainly well looked after, and he used to make me jealous when he talked about the regular warm baths he enjoyed. (A bath was something that, up until that time, was outwith the range of my experience.) When I went in for him about six a.m. it was like going from one world to another, especially in the winter-time. I rose and dressed in a cold, dark room. With only a paraffin lamp for light, I ate my breakfast, which consisted of a mug of tea and a couple of slices of bread and jam. All in all the scene had an aura of Dickensian austerity. What a difference when I entered my brother's home! From an old-fashioned, dark unheated house, I entered a gleaming, electrically-heated and lit room, filled with the lovely aroma of newly toasted bread. His woollen helmet and gloves were nicely warmed and his every comfort was catered for.

Every day, rain or shine, we walked the two miles to meet the cart. Sometimes we reached the farm before the milkroundsman had left, and it was nice in the winter mornings to get a heat from the stove in the bottle-washing shed. But I really loved the warm, balmy, summer mornings. The sun would rise above the Buckie Bin and kiss the dancing waves of the Moray Firth. The birds would break into their dawn chorus and one felt glad to be alive as the gentle zephyrs wafted the smell of ozone in from the sea. On the other hand, the dark wintry mornings were sometimes very unpleasant. The frost sometimes bit our hands until they became so swollen that we couldn't carry the bottles. We were often soaked to the skin before we even met the cart. Not only had we to finish our round like that but we sometimes ended up at school in the same way. There is in youth, however, a certain resilience which enables one to shrug off the unpleasant aspects of a particular task, so I had no wish to complain.

After all there were many compensating features. There were for instance the many exciting incidents with temperamental horses. When a horse bolted there would be enough excitement to last for a long time. We would follow the trail of strewn crates of milk and eventually catch up with the terrified animal. On at least two occasions I can remember our horse bolting in this way, and finding it injured in some cul-de-sac with the remnants of a milk-cart scattered around it. One horse belonging to a rival dairy, bolted down the steep brae in the centre of Buckie. The poor animal, driven with fear, ran headlong down, scattering crates of milk as it went. It was unable to negotiate the sharp bend of the embankment, with the result that it tried to jump the metal fence at the bottom, being horribly impaled on the spikes in the process. Needless to say it died midst this scene of carnage.

My brother and I were both fond of animals. Apart from the monkey, we had, as stated, every conceivable type of animal and bird, tame and otherwise. When you have the choice of the best vegetable gardens in the town at six a.m. at your disposal, then it isn't difficult to see that our rabbits and so on were fed on the very best. If we needed any materials for hutches or bird lofts, then we acquired it very early in the morning, hid them somewhere handy, and collected them later at night. If we needed a sledge and knew where there was one lying in some back garden, then some youngster discovered that his sledge had been spirited away during the night. In this way we obtained the best of wheels for our "cairties", and it didn't give us the slightest twinge of conscience to think that some youngster would be mourning their loss in some other part of the town. But just as sin starts in a small way and becomes worse and worse, so our practice of taking what did not belong to us gradually reached a more serious level. One is too ashamed to relate the details, but suffice it to say that in the more serious matters, restitution has been made.

My early childhood, as can be seen, was one continuous round of physical activity, interspersed with the fleeting moment of serious reflection. I had never been one to read books or to give myself to any concentrated study. I discovered, through sharing reading-books at school, that my reading speed was considerably slower than the average pupil. I usually pretended that I had finished the page to the one I was sharing the book with, rather than admit that I was so slow. Consequently I soon lost the trend of the story and gave up altogether, under the pretence that it was boring. I can only recall reading two library books during my years at school. Of course I took a book out of the school library regularly and claimed that I had read it but in actual fact it only gathered dust at home. Through no fault of her own, Grannie couldn't motivate me at all. Late night activities in search of excitement, coupled with early work on the milkround meant that my school performance was not what it should have been, and I for one just couldn't have cared less.

As far as I was concerned, any success that I would have in life would be restricted to the physical plane.

Although I was very agile and certainly stronger than most of my age group, I was deeply conscious of being small for my age. The fact that my younger brother was at least half a head taller, seemed to accentuate my lack of height. To try to compensate for this, I often put on a show of bravado, and this didn't always go down well with my pals. Quarrels would often erupt and I suppose my first major fight developed from such a quarrel. I say "suppose" because I can't remember a thing about it. All I know is that my opponent was fourteen years of age and had left school, and I was about ten, and several stones lighter. In street fighting there were no rules of course. This hulk of a lad had already gained a reputation for being tough, and he certainly came from a family renowned for fighting. Whilst I have no idea what led to this unequal contest taking place, I have no doubt that I had probably brought the David and Goliath situation on myself.

We had been playing football one summer's evening and had finished for the night. We gathered our jumpers and so on and prepared to go home. That's the last I can recall; the rest of the evening remains a blank. As I listened to my pals describing the fight to others at school the next day I was able to build up a picture of what had happened. The fight had lasted for a long time, neither of us being prepared to admit defeat.

Although I had taken a severe beating to begin with (and I had plenty of cuts and bruises to confirm the accuracy of that part of the story at least), I had refused to give in. To the great delight of my supporters, I slowly began to get the better of my antagonist. His strength slowly began to fail, whilst I, on the other hand, somehow managed to draw extra stamina from some hidden reserves. After a long gruelling battle I was declared the winner, and I became a hero overnight.

The problem about gaining a reputation, however, is that you must struggle to keep it. I rather foolishly basked in the sunshine of my new-found fame. It had brought me popularity, and it had given me a sense of belonging that I had never known before. I desperately wanted to cling on to this, but I little realised the terrible price I would have to pay to do so. I was careful not to mention the fact that I had been pummelled so badly about the head that a condition of complete amnesia had obliterated from my memory every detail of the fight. I didn't want to deprive myself of any glory, and so I gave my own version of a carefully-planned fight.

I have mentioned the price I had to pay. It was costly indeed, for more and more challenges were hurled at me from every quarter. Of course I couldn't back down after basking for weeks in the sunshine of popularity. I had a reputation to keep and fight I must. As each challenge was taken up, however, I found that I could anticipate my opponents' moves quite easily. Furthermore, part of my own individual physical chemistry was a built-in, exceptionally fast, reflex system. These two factors, plus a peak of fitness honed to perfection on a milkround, and a good sense of timing, I found to be the key to success. From merely fighting to keep a reputation, I graduated to fighting for the sheer pleasure of it.

With each fight I became more confident and the old adage proved to be true in my case: "success breeds success". It was a wonderfully exhilarating feeling to be superbly fit and to enjoy the adulation of your own peer group. I became a keep-fit fanatic, concentrating on building up my speed and stamina. The milk-round became an integral part of my keep-fit programme. The training routines of other athletes were assiduously studied and copied. Although most of my companions smoked, I abstained from this habit in order to keep in good condition. In fact I developed an abhorrence for the habit that has remained with me since.

# Chapter 8

## RUNAWAY

What triggered off the matter I don't know, but I gradually developed about this period, a strong desire to see my mother and father, and the rest of the family. Our family had now grown to six boys and one girl, some of whom I had never seen. My older brothers I knew only by name, having not seen them for many years. I received snatches of information about them through letters sent to Grannie from other relatives who also lived in Fleetwood. From an almost imperceptible urge to see them, the desire reached the proportion of an irresistible obsession. For some reason or other, I began to doubt Grannie's account of my being in Buckie and separated from my parents. In fact I began to suspect that she was keeping me away from them against their wishes. Once this seed of doubt was sown, it didn't take long for the notion to reach full bloom. The urge to see my parents to get the truth of the matter, finally reached a climax, and I decided to run away from home.

I knew of course that my grandparents on my mother's side lived in Portsoy. Somehow or other I felt that I would have to head there to begin with. I hadn't been there since I was a young child, and I couldn't remember a thing about the actual journey. All that I could remember was that Portsoy was on the coast. I had a vague mental picture of my grandparents' cottage, and felt that I could remember where it was once I reached the town. With this rather sketchy information I started to form my plans. First of all I started to influence my younger brother John. I confided in him about my suspicions, and went on to fill his mind with all sorts of foolish notions. He was, and with good cause, very happy in his own surroundings, and he hadn't the slightest inclination to leave the only mother that he had ever known. In fact he called her "mother" whilst Grannie just got called "Grannie" from me. Gradually, however, I managed to persuade him to join me in running away from home.

It was a beautiful morning when we set off. The sea was an azure blue, and there wasn't a breath of wind to disturb the glassy shimmer of the water. Indeed the day proved to be the hottest of the whole summer. We had noticed the tar melting on the road, even with the early morning sun, as we went on our milkround earlier on. Without telling anyone about our intentions we headed eastwards along the railway line. We passed Portessie, Findochty, Portknockie and then approached Cullen, always keeping a wary eye open for approaching trains. We need not have worried too much about them, however, for on such a beautiful day their approach could be heard fully a mile away.

We scrambled down the grassy embankment before we came to the Cullen viaducts, and then made our way through the Seatown part of the town. By this time we were absolutely ravenous with hunger. We drank from the burn that flows under the main viaduct, but we had no money to buy any food. The journey was proving to be much longer than I had anticipated, and I began to be a little concerned. Then I had an idea. I had once visited an old lady in Seatown along with a school friend. If we could find her little cottage perhaps she would give us something to eat. Those who have visited Cullen will know that the Seatown is a town-planner's nightmare, and it was only with great difficulty that I managed to recognise her quaint little home. In fact if it hadn't been for an unusual brass handle on the door, I doubt if I would have been able to find it. This had drawn my attention on my previous visit, and it was certainly a welcome sight on that scorching summer's day. Knocking on the door, we were welcomed by an old-fashioned lady. We spun a yarn about the purpose of our being in Cullen, but I felt that it didn't sound very convincing. However, we didn't need to drop a hint about being hungry, for the kind old soul had the kettle on right away. Soon we were wolfing down thick slices of bread, laced with the most delicious homemade raspberry-jam that I have ever tasted.

Bidding farewell to our benefactor we made more plans about the remainder of our journey. Some old fishermen were seated beside the little harbour enjoying the warm sunshine, and we thought we should ask directions of them about the best road to Portsoy. Although they readily supplied us with answers to our questions, I felt that they were a little suspicious. When they started asking us questions in return, I felt that it was time for us to be on our way. Instead of going by road as they had suggested, we decided to keep to the coastline. We were worried in case these fishermen would inform the police about us. It would have been an easy matter to pick us up on the main road, and so we set off along the rocky shore. The smell of paint and tar filled the air and gave us a heady feeling, and looking back across the bay we marvelled at the beauty of the unfamiliar scenery. The Bow-Fiddle rock at Portknockie melted in the intense heat haze. But we hadn't run away to enjoy a sightseeing tour, so we pushed on.

We hadn't travelled far along this coastline, with its sweeping shingle bays and small rocky cliffs, when we realised that we had made a big mistake. We knew the tortuous route was adding miles to our journey. Walking on the loose gravel and stumbling up rocky paths soon tired us out. The remorseless sun continued to beat down upon us, and we had to sit down and rest for a few minutes. Off we set again, fully expecting to see Portsoy after rounding each little headland, only to be disappointed time and time again.

"Let's head inland and link up with the main road, or maybe the railway line," I suggested, trying to hide the note of panic in my voice.

This decision led to one of the biggest frights of my life. After scaling the grassy bank of the raised beach, we were confronted with a high chain-link fence.

"Probably to stop the livestock from falling on to the rocks," I commented as I pushed my way through an opening.

I spotted a sign a little distance ahead. Thinking it would give us a clue as to our whereabouts, we ran to see what it had to say. We froze in our tracks. The bold letters, "WAR DEPARTMENT, DANGER, KEEP OUT", sent a chill down my spine. For fully a minute we stared blankly at the ominous message, hardly daring to breathe.

"I think we are in a minefield," I whispered in a rather tremulous voice. My brother looked at me with a questioning look on his face. A wave of regret swept over me — regret for thinking up the idea of running away from home — regret for persuading my brother to come with me. What a mess I had landed both of us in! As a kind of paralysing numbness took control of my nervous system, I recalled vividly the sun glinting off the two coffins of the young Portgordon boys. One of those I've-been-here-before feelings, made the hair at the back of my neck stiffen. Sheer terror made me almost vomit. Two self-confident runaways were, in a moment of time, reduced to two little frightened children.

Almost whimpering with fear, I told my brother to retrace his footsteps, making sure that he placed his feet gently on exactly the same spots that he had stood on as he entered. Without exchanging another word, we gingerly retraced our steps towards the hole in the fence. In what seemed an eternity, we wormed our way through and threw ourselves down on to the grassy bank, drained of energy, drenched in sweat, and overcome with emotion.

I've never been able to find out whether or not our fears were justified, but that has made no difference of course to the horror of our experience. Although the war had ended a couple of years prior to the event, there were still several minefields along the coast, each cordoned off to protect the public, until the mines were removed. I was convinced that we had landed right in the middle of one, and whether or not I was right is beside the point. For me it was an experience that I'll never forget. Strangely enough, eternal matters never entered my head during the whole episode, just the dreadful fear of being physically blown to smithereens.

After we had recovered somewhat from our ordeal, we walked along the beach until we came to the ruins of a castle, perched on the brow of a sheer cliff. Why anyone would want to build a castle on such a precarious position I just couldn't imagine. The crumbling ruins, even in brilliant sunshine, had a solemn, daunting look about them. It struck me that even in its heyday the building must have looked extremely forbidding. I learned later that it was the famous Findlater Castle, the reputed scene of a great human tragedy that has found a firm place in local folklore.

Striking inland from this point, we soon came

across signs of life. We asked a farmer for some directions, and soon we were on the high road, footsore and weary, but at least knowing where we were. We passed the road that coiled its way down to the picturesque little village of Sandend. By this time we were both suffering from a mild touch of sunstroke, and beginning to feel miserable. We stopped at another farmhouse at the side of the road and asked for a drink of water. The lady told us that we had just about a mile to walk, and right enough, around the bend of the road we could see a church spire. Portsoy at last!

We decided to make for the harbour, for we knew that our grandparents lived a short distance from it. I could visualise in my mind the long, low cottage we had visited along with our parents some seven years earlier. As we drew near to the harbour, the mental picture from the past began to fit the present scene. There was the basin with its crystal clear water, and the little, neatly painted lobster and mackerel boats. There was the little brae leading up to their cottage. We felt very conspicuous as we sauntered along the side of the harbour. Dozens of youngsters were splashing around in the shallow end of the basin. Some of them stared at us as we passed by. Our first impulse was to go and bathe our aching feet in the water, but we decided to go to our grandparents and announce our arrival first of all.

On our way up the brae, we were delighted to see a little monkey, just like Tarzie, fastened to a lead and sitting on a shed. The neat little shed had obviously been specially made for it, and was placed right on the edge of the bank, where it could watch all the activity around the harbour. It was watching at that moment the children enjoying themselves in the water. It became excited when we approached, and we stopped for a while to watch its antics. Unlike our poor, unfortunate Tarzie, this sleek-coated animal was obviously being well looked after.

Feeling the hunger pangs once again reminded me that we should make for the cottage without any further delay. I was becoming a little apprehensive by this time, but I did not convey my true feelings to my brother. For one thing what were we going to say? I had been trying all the way to Portsoy to formulate in my mind a convincing explanation for running away from Buckie, but I just couldn't verbalise my inner feelings. I took a deep breath and knocked on the cottage door.

After a few faltering attempts to introduce ourselves, we were ushered in and made very welcome. In no time a substantial meal was set before us, and we didn't require a lot of coaxing to get our teeth into it. A group of young children gathered shyly around the open door and giggled and pushed each other. These, we were told, were some of our many cousins from Portsoy. They all wanted to get a glimpse of their Buckie relations. This made us feel uneasy, as if we were a couple of strange exhibits. We were glad when an uncle told them all to run away and play elsewhere. He also suggested that we should go down to the

harbour and freshen ourselves up with a swim.
Our protests that we didn't have a swimming
costume were swept aside. We were both handed
a pair of girls' knickers and were told that this
was the standard costume for a boy in Portsoy.
When we realised that we wouldn't be conspicuous
oddities, we gladly took them and headed for the
cool waters of the harbour to douse our tired,
travel-weary bodies. In no time at all we were
completely refreshed and enjoying ourselves, the
trials of the journey for the time being forgotten.

We were still paddling about an hour later
when the same uncle came down to tell us that a
policeman was at the cottage and wanted to see
us. Sheepishly we headed up the brae past the
jibbering monkey. The policeman towered above
us as he plied us with questions. As he spoke in a
very grave tone of voice and wrote down some of
our answers in a little book, I began to feel like a
criminal — especially as the full responsibility of
the escapade rested on my older shoulders.

After lengthy discussions between the policeman
and various relatives who had appeared from
nowhere, we were given a cup of tea and some
biscuits. My grandfather took us up to the bus
stop, put us on a Buckie-bound bus and paid our
fares. He told the conductress to make sure we got
off at Buckie, and off we set in an old Alexander's
"bluebird" bus. As we headed westwards, the sun,
like a glowing orb of fire, sank below the horizon
to announce the end of another day. But what a
day!

On the way home we didn't say much to each

other. I quietly mused over the events of the day. Feelings of anger began to well up within me. I thought of the difficulty I had faced as I attempted to explain our reasons for running away. I knew my arguments didn't sound very satisfactory. But I had a reason. Why hadn't they listened to me?

"You've a good home, Charles," they had told me, and yet I knew that they had never been inside my home.

"Look how big and strong John is. Picture of health isn't he? Must be well nourished." Even the policeman had nodded his agreement. As far as he was concerned we were just a little report in his little book. We had probably been just an amusing interlude in an otherwise monotonous day. What I had wanted to scream at them was the fact that we didn't just want a good home; we didn't just want warm clothes, good food and a nice bed. What we wanted more than anything else in the whole wide world was a mother's love! We wanted a sense of identity — we wanted to experience for once in our lives a sense of belonging. Speaking for myself, I know I would gladly have suffered hunger, poverty, in fact any hardship imaginable, if only I could become part of our family. Had I been an orphan I would have accepted our situation, but I had a real father and mother, and I yearned for their love and care. I wanted to be with them, but no one seemed to understand my emotional dilemma, and now all my plans had been frustrated.

The driver changed to a lower gear and the old

bus groaned its way up the steep brae at Buckie.
Pulling violently on the steering wheel, he
swerved around the memorial and made his
brakes squeal as he brought his bus to a halt at the
bus-stop. Then I saw Grannie and my aunt
waiting for us with dark scowls on their faces. We
pretended not to see them and decided to wait
until we reached the Buckpool stop. The
conductress had not forgotten my grandfather's
instructions, however, and she told us to get off. I
was about to explain that Buckpool was where we
were heading for when Grannie spotted our
reluctance to get off. Boarding the bus, she
bellowed at the top of her voice for us to leave the
bus at once. We didn't require a second shout.

Being older than my brother meant, of course,
that I was branded as the villain of the escapade.
There was absolutely no doubt in anybody's mind
that they were right, and no attempt was made on
my part to deny the fact. But sad to say they
rubbed this in to such an extent that I rapidly
came to one conclusion, and that was to run away
again as soon as possible. This time I would
definitely go alone. Instead of trying to find out
the cause of my unusual behaviour, Grannie,
rather foolishly, adopted a threatening attitude
in an attempt to prevent a recurrence. There
were no child-guidance clinics in those days to
give suitable advice. Grannie just did what she
thought was right, but it was obviously the wrong
approach altogether. Within days I was planning
to run away from the only home I'd known, but as
far as I was concerned, there would be no coming

back.

The summer holidays had just ended, and the transition from Primary to Secondary school had just taken place. All my school chums were excited about the wide range of new subjects to which they had just been introduced. But I wasn't the slightest bit concerned, because I knew I wouldn't be in Buckie much longer.

I chose a Sunday for my second bid. I had enough money to get to Cullen by bus. From Cullen I took the main coastal road to Portsoy. The day was quite cool and I was young and fit. It didn't take me long therefore to reach Portsoy. I had jogged for considerable stretches of the road, and I couldn't help comparing the ease of the journey with the arduous strain of the previous one.

By the time I reached the outskirts of the town it was late afternoon. There appeared to be no-one about as I proceeded down to the now familiar cottage. Once inside I was faced with a barrage of questions. More relatives gathered and there were more questions. I made it clear in a surly, determined voice, that I would not, under any circumstances, return to Buckie. I let them see that they were wasting their time in trying to persuade me to go back. I had made up my mind that I was going to be reunited to my family, even if I had to walk every mile to Fleetwood.

I don't know exactly what went on behind the scenes that evening, but it was fairly obvious that frantic calls were made to Buckie to inform my grandparents of my arrival, and also to

Fleetwood, to let my mother know about the problems I had created by my behaviour. I was informed later that night that my mother had decided to come up by train and bring me down to the family home. At long last my fondest dreams were coming true. I would soon be on my way home. As I lay in bed that night I was in such a state of euphoria that I just couldn't sleep. I had never been able to address anyone as "mother" or "father" before. Would I say "mam" or "dad"? I chuckled to myself as I pondered over such childish trivialities. Only one thing blighted my complete happiness, and that was the fact that I would be leaving my brother John behind in Buckie. Circumstances had drawn us very close together, and I certainly knew that we would miss each other. Some time during the small hours of the morning I finally fell into a peaceful sleep.

The next two days were spent rambling around the harbour and the rocky shore. My grandfather had a mackerel boat, and he showed me how to tie on the hooks to the line. I spent a lot of time near to the monkey's shed. Some of my relatives invited me to their homes, but it soon became obvious to everyone that I was anxious to start my journey south.

My mother arrived just after teatime one evening. She was tired and rather irritable after the long train journey. The little, dark-haired woman, wasn't just what I had imagined her to be. Her habit of chain-smoking revolted me, and there was no display of emotion or affection when she met me. I had prepared myself for something quite different. In fact there were no emotional feelings on my part towards her. It was all a bit of an anti-climax for me. I had wondered how I would manage to cope in an emotional situation, for I had never been one for openly displaying my deeper feelings. The woman who was called my mother was nothing more than a stranger. I began to feel embarrassed as she started to make angry comments about the extortionate prices being charged for railway tickets, the many changes of trains she had to make, draughty stations, and the worry of having to leave the rest of the family at home. I tried to analyse once again that night, as I lay in bed staring at the ceiling, my reasons for running away. My eyes shimmered with tears as I indulged in a bout of self-pity, trying to convince myself that I had at least deserved some reassurance from my own mother that I had done the right thing. But as I recalled all that she had said that day, I couldn't think of a word that could have been interpreted as being encouraging. Quite the reverse. To this stranger with the half-Scots, half-English accent, I was nothing more than a problem, a nuisance.

Next day a small group gathered on the tiny railway-station platform. The steam train chugged its way along the line towards us, spewing out smoke and steam. Once inside, the window was lowered and the farewells were said. As the metal monster pulled away from the huddled group of waving relatives, I felt strangely uncomfortable being left alone with my mother. I just couldn't bring myself to converse with her directly. When she tried to engage me in conversation I felt tongue-tied, and confined my answers to "yes" and "no". The journey itself seemed to take an age. I just stared out of the window at the speeding, changing scenery. Big, ugly factories with smoking chimneys sped past. Then there were endless miles of mist-covered moorlands. Then I spotted a school caught in the process of disgorging its blazer-clad pupils. My thoughts went immediately to my old school at Buckie. I wondered what my teachers were saying about my absence. The faintest trace of a smile appeared at the corner of my mouth as I visualised the daily attendance ritual.

"Anyone know what's wrong with Charles Geddes?"

"Yes Miss, he's run away from home."

I felt a warm feeling of pride well up within me as I convinced myself that this latest escapade would place me even higher in the esteem of my chums.

The train rattled on. "Taking you home, taking you home, taking you home," the rhythm of the wheels seemed to be telling me, as we sped on through the gathering gloom. Every mile was bringing me nearer my brothers and sister. "Taking you home, taking you home," the train seemed to pick up my thoughts and share in my mounting excitement. Then sleep finally overtook me as my head vibrated against the corner of the window.

"We change here!" For the fourth time I had

been given that information. Earlier on in the journey it had been very exciting, but by now the novelty had worn off. As if in a dream, I saw the hurrying masses of people. Hissing engines stood as if angry with the delay. Strange accents punctuated the jarring cacophany that was dominated by a booming voice, telling everyone where a certain train on a certain platform was heading for, and the time of departure. There were so many trains in the massive station that I was sure that every train in the country must have gathered for some special reason.

After a mad rush from one platform to another, I found myself in yet another train. I was assured that it was the last one, and that our next stop would be Fleetwood. This news drove all sleep from my eyes. I was almost home! The first streaks of dawn were playing on the eastern sky as we entered the station of Lancashire's famous fishing port. Buckie seemed a million miles away. Everything seemed so strange and different. All the buildings were made of brick, and not of stone as was the case in Buckie and district. I had never seen a man wearing clogs before, but now I saw dozens of them hurrying past on their way to their work at the fishing docks. Even at that early hour there was an atmosphere of intense activity. My brothers and sister were, however, still in bed when we arrived at my new home.

They made me very welcome, although they teased me a lot about my Scottish accent. Even my mother seemed a lot happier now that the journey was over. I was taken to all the various places of amusement down on the promenade. Down at the docks I was shown the massive trawlers, and I was surprised to see how buckled the plates were on quite a number of them. It was obvious that during their long trips to the Icelandic waters they had taken some severe poundings. I thought of my father who was fishing there at that very moment, and who was due home in about a couple of weeks' time.

Then there was the glorious day at Blackpool. We went there by tramcar and spent the whole day going round the many attractions. The tower and the huge swimming pool were the places that appealed to me most. Nagging at the pit of my stomach, however, was the thought that we had a brother away far north, who should have been with us enjoying himself. He would be at school whilst we were still on holiday, because the school session started later in Fleetwood.

As the days went by, I began to sense that my mother was getting a little uneasy. This was more noticeable when any reference was made about my father's expected arrival from sea, so I naturally associated the one with the other.

"Dad's ship's arrived mum! Saw it coming up the river!" It was my oldest brother Jimmie. He was always in the vicinity of the docks, or the river Wyre that weaves its way from the docks to the open sea. He knew all about the arrival and departure of the trawlers, and invariably brought home the news that my father's ship had arrived.

I was watching my mother's reactions carefully

as the exciting news was joyfully proclaimed. Contrary to my expectations, there was no sign of pleasure on her face. There was just the same strained look that I had noticed in recent days. I just couldn't fathom the possible reason for this unusual attitude. I could understand, in measure her impatience and bad temper after making what, I now realised, was an extremely gruelling train journey north. I decided to stay in the background and keep a low profile until I saw what was what.

I was sitting reading the paper in the living room, when the shouts of my brothers at the back of the house announced that my father was coming up the cobbled back-alley. I just remained where I was, pretending to read, but really too excited to do anything but listen. My mother was in the kitchen at the rear of the house so I was glad to be out of the way meantime. My father's jovial voice greeted my brothers, and soon they were all in the kitchen. I became deeply aware that the happy babble had subsided to almost a whisper. My mother's subdued voice was describing the recent events. My father started firing questions at her, and she was appealing to him to keep his voice down. Sometimes she herself spoke loudly in defence of what she had done. For me the tension became almost unbearable. This was the moment that I'd longed for. In my dreams I'd seen my father sweeping me into his arms and telling me how proud he was to welcome me back into the family circle. Now the moment of fulfilment had arrived.

The door opened slowly and the stranger I knew to be my father entered the room. I put down the paper and looked him straight in the eye. Not a sound came from the kitchen, and time itself seemed to stand still as we held each other's gaze. A thousand emotions swept over me, but I just didn't know what to say or what to do. A baffled runaway, searching for parental affection, I sat motionless, waiting for my father to speak.

"You shouldn't have come!" His words stunned me. I sat completely speechless, unable to take in the full implication of the statement. Such was my state of shock, that his following statements just didn't penetrate my understanding. Everything that I'd hoped for, longed for, and secretly wept for, was now being brutally torn away from me. I wanted to cry out in sheer desperation "But I'm your son, don't you remember?" but my vocal cords had seized up. In a trance-like state, I could now make out his ramblings about the "good home I had", and about how "Grannie would be missing me". He seemed to be talking to me from a great distance, and as he did so, his voice seemed to resurrect emotions, dreams, impressions of childhood, and blend them together into a confusing jigsaw before my mind. This was too much for me to cope with, so I made a hasty retreat to the privacy of my bedroom to give vent to my feelings. There alone, with tears cascading down my cheeks, and fists pounding against the pillow, I was completely overwhelmed by a sense of loneliness and despair. Biting my lips to stifle massive sobs that welled up from the pit of my stomach, I was consumed by the unspeakable horror of alienation. I didn't belong to anyone. I didn't fit in anywhere. Nobody cared. For all the importance I was to anyone, I might as well have not existed. I was nobody, in fact worse than nobody, for I was now branded as superfluous and a nuisance.

Somewhere in the middle of this orgy of self-pity, my feelings began to change. The fighting instinct began to take control. I was back to the summer's evening, fighting a power far too big for me, but I wasn't going to give in. I would fight and fight and fight. Mentally the savage blows were saying "Give in," but something else, call it pride or madness, said "Fight on". I could closely-hear the wheels of the train, this time in mockery, "Taking you home, taking you home, taking you home", and blind hate for everyone and everything, began to eat into my very soul. Pounding the bed in a frenzy of unharnessed fury, I whispered my hatred of my mother and father, using vile language dredged up from the gutter of my wounded heart. In between convulsive sobs, I bemoaned the fact that I had ever been born. My parents had rejected me, their own son, their own flesh and blood. They had shattered all my cherished hopes, and destroyed the only thing that I had wanted in life, and that was to belong to a family and feel secure. They had now made it abundantly clear that they hadn't a spark of remorse for what they had done to me as a two year old. Grannie had been right after all. The cold, callous truth had at last to be faced. During that traumatic hour, lying on that tear-soaked bed, I think I mentally "came of age". I went to the bathroom, washed my face and went downstairs determined that neither they nor anyone else would ever make me cry again.

The weeks passed, but I didn't go to school. It was obvious that my parents didn't want to enrol me, and I wasn't too sure that I wanted to go in any case. It was obvious that my father had a drink problem, and it was just as well that he was off to the sea on long trips most of the time. Drinking and gambling filled his days ashore, and I never got close to him. Something had to be done about me, but there didn't seem to be any solution to the problem. I had retreated into a kind of morose shell, becoming very reluctant to express my thoughts. No doubt my parents salved their consciences by thinking I was pining for Buckie.

The problem was solved, as far as my parents were concerned, through a letter sent from an aunt in Buckie. In heart-rending terms, she described my grandfather's great affection for me, and how my absence was breaking his heart. She went on to say that he was extremely ill, and that if I wanted to see him before he died, I would have to go to Buckie without delay. My mother played on this and I soon began to blame myself for his illness. To her thinly-veiled delight, I announced that I wanted to go back to my grandparents for good. I genuinely wanted to see my grandfather before he died, for I realised that I had misjudged him by running away, and now I knew he was one of the few who had ever shown me any real kindness. Again the long journey was undertaken, and I found myself back north, two months after running away.

It turned out that my aunt's tear-jerking pleadings, and claims about the seriousness of my grandfather's illness, were grossly exaggerated. But that didn't make any difference now, for I was glad to be home. I was no longer deceived. I saw my grandparents in an entirely new light. They had sacrificed for me in order to make up for the irresponsibility of others. But I was also a very young boy, having a very big chip on my shoulder. The disillusionment resulting from my runaway episode, had made me determined never to rely on anyone, no matter who they were. I was going to make my own way in life. I didn't need parents. In fact I didn't need anyone at all.

# Chapter 9

## BOXING DAFT

Going back to school was a bewildering experience. All my school companions were fairly well versed by this time in such complex subjects as algebra and geometry. They spoke about $H_2O$ and theorems with an air of authority. Needless to say, I hadn't a clue about what they were talking. Had there been Guidance staff at our school at that time, they would have realised that I had two closely-related problems. Firstly, I had come through a traumatic experience and required a lot of sympathetic, supportive help to enable me to adjust. In other words I had a deep emotional problem. My second problem was an academic one. Because of absenteeism, I had missed the vital introduction to a wide range of subjects. This meant that, without special help, I would never be able to catch up with, and keep abreast of, my colleagues. No extra help was offered and I lagged behind throughout my three year of Secondary school. I just drifted through, totally disinterested and longing for the day when I could leave. I can't think of anything that I learned whilst there, and it is certain that I didn't contribute a thing towards the well-being of the school. As far as I was concerned, it was all a complete waste of time for the teachers and myself. I had paid the price for running away.

I had been back in Buckie about nine months when my grandfather's condition began to deteriorate rapidly. He suffered a lot towards the end from his chronic bronchitis. It was heart-rending to watch him gasping for air and coughing up mouthfuls of phlegm. Relatives had been sent for, and our house was overcrowded. I slept among the herring nets in a make-shift bed, in order to give mine to others. I was wakened one morning to be told that he had passed away during the night. I had mixed feelings about the news. I was glad that he was no longer suffering from his chest trouble, but at the same time I was sorry to lose one who had been so kind and understanding when I was a nervous little boy. Indeed, I realised at that moment that I'd lost the only father I'd ever known.

The coffin was placed in the living-room. I can vividly remember gazing upon the waxen face of my grandfather. Had it not been for his trim white moustache, I probably wouldn't have recognised him. He looked so serene after his many years of racking pain. The lid of the coffin leaned against the wall, the brass plate bearing his name and age striking me as odd. "After all, what good would that information be once you were six feet under the ground?" I mused.

On the day of the funeral the house was crammed with people. During the short service they sang my grandfather's favourite hymn:

"There's a land that is fairer than day,
And by faith we can see it afar;
And the Father waits over the way,
To prepare us a dwelling place there.
In the sweet ... by-and-by,
We shall meet on that beautiful shore,
In the sweet ... by-and-by,
We shall meet on that beautiful shore".

I had never heard such singing in my life, and the words were deeply moving. I stood beside the open coffin, trying in vain to keep back the tears. I wondered if I would ever meet my grandfather again on a "beautiful shore". As I looked at the wasted frame, wrapped now in a death shroud, the very idea seemed an utter impossibility. The hymn was surely sentimental, wishful thinking — something to soften the blow for the mourners. Death was ugly, hideous, but worst of all final. The tears came freely now as the undertaker screwed down the coffin lid. I had lost forever a good friend.

I brooded over the finality of death on the way to the cemetery and on the way home I expressed my thoughts to an older companion. I was quite surprised by his comments.

"Well, you know what the Bible has to say about it don't you?"

I didn't know, and my attitude towards the Bible was usually negative. But my heart was a little tender that day, and I was prepared to encourage his conversation.

"No, I don't know; what does it say?"

"Well it says, 'Let us eat and drink; for tomorrow we die.' You see," he continued, "that simply means that we are expected to enjoy ourselves as long as we are able. We haven't to brood over the passing away of others. Our time to die will come soon enough, and it's up to us to make the best of the life that God has given to us."

This made sense to me. I began to think that the Bible wasn't full of rubbish after all. What I didn't know was that the words quoted by the young man had been taken out of their context. The Apostle Paul, I learned later, had written these words to the believers at Corinth to show how futile it was to suffer as a Christian, if, as some false teachers were trying to assert, there was no resurrection. They were part of his lucid argument in favour of this most important truth. They were certainly not written to give God's approval to lives of self-indulgence. But, of course, I didn't know this at the time. The Bible was still a closed book to me.

It was just after this sad event that my attention was caught by an interesting article in our local weekly newspaper. It was all about a local hairdresser, Bill Forbes by name, but better known as "Lightning Bill". In his younger days he had gained quite a reputation as a clever, stylish boxer. The highlight of his boxing career was undoubtedly his bout with the Imperial Champion of the Navy, Army and Air Force at a gala in Buckie in 1936. Bill had only a few minutes to spare, as he hadn't dared to ask time off from his work. The first round had barely started when a lethal punch from Bill connected with the Champion's jaw and knocked him unconscious.

Said Bill, "I was on my way down to the hairdresser's shop where I worked, before the poor chap was on his feet. In fact the Navy Commodore had been in the process of lighting his cigar when the fight started, and he missed the whole thing".

During the war, Bill had been a P.T. instructor in the Navy, and he was an expert at unarmed combat. Now in his early forties, he was still a keep-fit fanatic. There was no doubt that he epitomised everything that I wanted to be myself. Now, claimed the article in the newspaper, Bill wanted to start a boxing-club in the town. Any youngster who was interested, had to be at the Territorial Hall at seven p.m. on the following Friday. As I gazed at the photograph of this great sportsman with his rippling muscles, my mind was already made up to be there.

Friday just couldn't come quickly enough for me. I was the first member to be enrolled, having stood for an hour before the appointed time.

Bill spotted my enthusiasm right away, and from the very start he took a personal interest in me. Every week he would give me some helpful advice about how to improve my boxing skills.

"I don't want any public-house brawling," he would say, and then go on to show what he meant by the scientific approach to boxing. He had no time for those who smoked and drank, for they showed, as far as he was concerned, a lack of commitment to the sport. His enthusiasm was infectious, and I found myself almost idolising the man. I used a part of our net loft as a mini-gymnasium, and regularly practised every routine that Bill had passed on to me. Training sessions became an obsession with me. I would shadow-box holding heavy lumps of lead in my hands. I was a glutton for roadwork and thought nothing about running about five or six miles of an evening. There was nothing I enjoyed more than sparring with the other members of the club on a Friday night.

In my first actual inter-club contest, my opponent had to give up in the middle of the second round, and I was successfully launched on an amateur career that was to last for the next seven years. The sport gave me the opportunity to

Front Right: A very young member of the boxing team.

give vent to all my pent-up aggression in a controlled situation. There can be no doubt at all that this acted as a timely safety-valve in my case, for one shudders to think what serious trouble my emotional hang-ups could have led me into. But another bitter blow was soon to fall, and to a youth with my particular zest for sport, it was very distressing indeed.

It was during our P.T. class at school, when we stripped to the waist, that someone said I had some spots on my back. The gym-teacher had a look and advised me to go to my doctor to have it checked out. That evening I went to see our family doctor.

"Mmmmm. Nasty," he muttered as his finger traced a crazy pattern over my back.

"Yes, well then ...," he continued, as his pen scratched across the prescription pad. "A touch of psoriasis I'm afraid."

"Psoriasis!" The word was entirely new to me. "What on earth's that?" I asked myself.

"Just apply this ointment twice a day and come back to see me in a fortnight," he said in a matter of fact way that was reassuring.

I left the surgery thinking that I had contracted something like measles or chickenpox, something that would disappear in a few day's time. Although the condition was very stubborn to begin with, it gradually began to clear up. After a few visits to the doctor there wasn't a spot to be seen. I was very relieved because I had been forced to opt out of the P.T. classes because of some of the comments made by other pupils, who were afraid that the disease was infectious.

It didn't hamper my training schedule, however, but since the boxing season was about to begin, I was anxious to get rid of these annoying scaly spots. There was no recurrence of the trouble that winter, and I gladly dismissed the matter from my mind as having been some belated childhood skin infection. I got on with the boxing, travelling to every corner of the north-east of Scotland with the club. Boxing is, of course, an individualistic sport, where you must take all the blame if you lose. On the other hand, you alone receive the credit if you win. There is no sharing of the glory with other members of a team, and this gave the sport for me an added attraction. Soon the trophies began to accumulate, and of these I was very proud.

But the spots did reappear. I repeated my visits to the doctor and got the same tarry-smelling ointment, and carried out the same messy ritual each day. This time the spots were all over my arms and legs, as well as on my back. I cannot even begin to describe my feelings of distress, when I began to realise the true nature of the disease. I began to notice advertisements in various publications about it, and how it could be cured if the patient used a special course of treatment. Unknown to anyone, I was to spend every spare penny I had during the following five years, buying supplies of this treatment.

Amateur boxers wear a vest during bouts, and therefore I could hide the spots on my chest and my back. I couldn't, of course, hide the spots on my legs and arms. On one occasion, the condition was so bad that I was too self-conscious to take part in a bout that had been arranged. Without giving any reasaon, I withdrew at the last minute. This surprised everyone, and when I gave some feeble excuse for opting out, they naturally suspected that I was afraid to meet my opponent. This just about broke my heart. It was bad enough to cope with the disease itself, but to be thought of as being a coward, was the worst injury that could have been inflicted on me. I was on the horns of a dilemma. I couldn't bring myself to say what my true reasons for backing out were, and yet the insinuations of cowardice were unbearable. Whilst my trainers knew that I was having a bit of trouble with my skin, they were unaware that it was gradually getting worse. The spots were in fact increasing in size and merging with others to form ugly patches. I was acutely aware of letting my club down, and it was made worse by the fact that, apart from my skin, I was in superb physical condition. I didn't go with the club to watch the tournament. I just couldn't fill the role of a spectator, so I stayed at home brooding.

At my grandfather's funeral, as stated, I had at least considered the possibility that there was a God, Who had given us our life, to be enjoyed to the full. Now I was absolutely certain that there was no God. A God in control of the universe would never allow this to happen. A God in control of the world would never allow all the suffering and wars to blight people's happiness.

He wouldn't stand back and be unconcerned about the inequality and unfairness regarding health and wealth. No, my own philosophy had been right: I was still that piece of flotsam floating on the sea of life, at the mercy of impersonal forces which carried me hither and thither, according to their capricious will. An extra wave of misfortune had ruffled things for me. A genetic joke had been played, and the laugh was on me. I was the smallest son of our family. I had recently discovered that I had defective colour-vision. Now I had a loathesome skin disease that had already robbed me of my self-respect. But I wasn't going to give in. I would fight on, and on, and on.

I left school when I was fifteen, without any qualifications of description. I was glad to leave and I'm sure my teachers were equally glad to see me go. Engineering took my fancy, so I went down to the local shipyard to apply for a job that had been advertised. A friend of mine who had just left school as well, went down with me to be interviewed for the job. I was called into the office first.

"Is your father a fisherman?" I was asked.

I had been expecting some form of intelligence test, and so I was quite surprised by the manager's approach. I was glad to tell him that my father was indeed a fisherman.

"Is he a skipper?" was the next question.

"No, he is an engineer on board a Fleetwood trawler," I replied, thinking that because my father was an engineer, this would be to my advantage.

"Oh, I see, Fleetwood you say. Oh well I'll let you know if anything opens up."

And that was it. No I.Q. tests. No concern about whether I could read or write. No questions about my school career or my technical skills. It was the strangest interview that one could imagine. My friend was called into the office, so I decided to wait for him. He came out grinning after a few minutes.

"Start my apprenticeship on Monday," he chirped. "When I told him my old man's the skipper of the *Campania* that clinched it."

This friend of mine had been in my class in the Secondary school for three years, and was no brighter than myself. Now here he was getting a job on the strength of his father owning a fishing-boat. No doubt the manager was now banking on getting all the repair work on this boat in the future. This was my first experience of discrimination, and it certainly left a sour taste in my mouth for a long time.

I got a full-time job on a milkcart and then got the opportunity to serve my apprenticeship as a builder. There was no choice in the matter. It was the first job to become available, and so I accepted it. It was a hard job and the handling of heavy concrete blocks, cement and lime, played havoc with my skin condition. I had to apply ointment continually to keep it under control, and that meant that in the winter months, I suffered terribly from the cold, as I worked outside in exposed building-sites. Every morning I had to apply the ointment, and the ritual was repeated at night. For the most part I was able to keep the trouble in check, and was able to take part in all the subsequent boxing tournaments. This made me quite popular with my workmates in the building squad. My progress was often the topic of conversation, and this gave me a warm feeling of satisfaction inside. The heavy work helped to build up the strength of my arms, and I continued to train as hard as ever.

Although I had heard that there was no cure for psoriasis, I refused to believe it. I kept on spending money on advertised forms of treatment, in the hope that I would finally be cured and prove the pessimists to be wrong. Like the woman in the Bible, of whom I learned later, instead of getting better, I grew worse.

Then a further interest began to make demands on my life. My brother John had bought an accordion, and had become quite an accomplished player. One day he suggested that I should learn to play some kind of instrument and help him form a little danceband. I had always liked the sound of a saxophone, so I decided to save up and buy a secondhand one. I got one for ten pounds and within a few months I had learned to play fairly acceptably, without any tuition of any description. We bartered an old three-wheeler car (which we had been unable to put on the road) for a set of drums. Soon our net-loft was vibrating with the sound of dance music as we practised for wedding dances and so on, for which we had received bookings. We had a very talented pianist to make up our four-piece band, and the engagements started to pour in.

One very amusing incident took place whilst on our way to an engagement in Portgordon. We had been unable to book our usual taxi, which had a roomy boot to accommodate all our instruments. In desperation we hired a taxi from a man who had just started up in business. He managed to put all the instruments in the boot apart from the big bass drum. As we were running late we began to panic a little. He eventually managed, however, to tie the drum to the roof of the vehicle, and off we went. Halfway along the mile-stretch of road towards Portgordon, I thought I heard a dull thump and told the driver to stop. In the semi-darkness we could just see the big drum

Left: In the band along with
my inseparable friend George.

rolling merrily on its way back to Buckie. We all laughed about it afterwards, but it certainly wasn't funny at the time. Needless to say, we made sure that we booked our usual taxi in good time after that incident.

To play the saxophone involves puckering the lips around the mouthpiece. The lips must obviously be in a healthy condition. I was still very much involved in the boxing scene, and this meant that my lips were sometimes in a messy condition. This, as can be realised, gave the band a bad image, as well as adversely affecting my musical performance. My brother was a bit of a perfectionist, and he expressed his annoyance on several occasions. I managed to carry on with both the danceband and the boxing activities, however, and so I really was burning the candle at both ends. I was never in bed before midnight, and sometimes it was nearer morning before we even got home.

Only those who have been actively involved in such activities, can understand something of the thrill of getting the crowd's approval. Whether it was the cheer of the crowd in a smoke-filled boxing hall, or the more restrained applause from a group of dancers, it was a tremendously invigorating experience. And yet, as time went past, there was the thought, the notion, the inner voice, call it what you will, telling me that the whole thing was empty and meaningless. I would shrug off such fleeting ideas and remind myself that "life was for living". I was getting on just

fine. I was carving out my own way in life, and I
didn't need anything else. Death, I realised, was a
spectre looming on the far-distant horizon. But it
was too far away for me to worry about it. I was
too busy getting on with the business of living to
worry about the business of dying. At least that is
what I tried to believe, until I met the spectre
face to face one Saturday afternoon.

# Chapter 10

## SEARCHING

Along with my brother, I had been invited to go sailing in a small boat, by the friend who had pipped me for the engineering job. He claimed that the boat was his, and we were delighted to go with him. He was a rather devil-may-care character, and was always getting into some mischief. Only the previous week, he and another youth had to be rescued by the local lifeboat, after their boat had been reported missing. They had drifted five miles out into the open sea, and were in danger of capsizing in the heavy swell. This had caused a bit of excitement in the town. The older generation, who had a healthy respect for the sea, condemned the foolhardy antics of the young adventurers. Here we were, however, going out of the harbour in the same little boat.

"Where's the oars?" I asked, looking around as our companion started to paddle with pieces of broken fish-boxes.

"They're locked up and I've forgotten to take the key. Come on, give us a hand, these boards will do just as well," he replied with a rather suspicious grin on his face.

All at once the air was filled with oaths and curses. A young man, his face livid with rage, was running along the quay, shouting at the top of his voice. He was the young man who had shared the drama in the previous week, and it was now obvious that he, and not our friend, was the owner of the boat. I thought he would take a fit when we obeyed our companion's instructions to ignore him. We drowned out his vehement threats by singing at the top of our voices: "A life on the ocean wave, a life on the ocean wave!"

"Watch yourselves out there boys, the wind's getting up."

The speaker was an old fisherman who was standing beside the white-painted lighthouse. We gave him a cheery wave but paid no attention to his warning. After all, we couldn't lose face by turning the boat around at that point, for the owner would assume that his threats had succeeded.

We had scarcely left the end of the breakwater, when the wind swept in from the north-west, and tugged violently at our small craft. Under normal circumstances we would have turned immediately and headed for the relative calm of the harbour. But the furious owner was still standing at the edge of the quay, hurling verbal abuse at us. Foolishly we decided to carry on.

Within a matter of minutes we were in real trouble. We couldn't control the boat with our makeshift oars. We were being swept along by the heavy swell towards the back of the harbour wall. We gave up trying to paddle, and held on for grim death. We were slowly driven nearer the massive wall where the waves were smashing themselves in a shower of spray. We knew that more than one ship had perished at the same spot in the past. With an onshore wind, our position was becoming critical. I can vividly recall being amazed at the height of the wall from our unenviable vantage point. A small group of onlookers had gathered at the top to watch the proceedings. We were in the inexorable clutches of the wind and waves, and we knew that within a few minutes our tiny craft would be smashed to driftwood. I had already taken off my shoes, and although mentally I knew that I couldn't swim well enough to survive in such turbulent waters, survival instincts prepared me to make an attempt. Then it happened. I prayed. Yes, I prayed silently that if there was a God, He would save us from the predicament that we had landed in.

The people on the wall started to point out to sea, but we couldn't see anything. They were shouting at us, but their words were being snatched away by the wind. Then we spotted the motor-powered mackerel boat heading for us. The fishermen had been making for the shelter of the harbour, and had noticed the people standing on the wall, and decided to come closer to investigate. Without a moment to spare, a rope was secured, and with a great deal of effort we were finally dragged to the safety of the harbour.

I don't know to this day why the lifeboat wasn't alerted. I can only surmise that it had happened so quickly, that we were probably hidden behind the high wall before the Coastguard men at the lookout a half-mile away could spot us. In any case it is doubtful whether they could have reached us in time. Be that as it may, what I do know is, that I was never so grateful to have my feet on terra-firma as I was on that occasion. Of course I didn't tell anyone how scared I had been, and I certainly never breathed a word about my silent prayer to God for help. But I HAD prayed, and that for the first time in my life. Somehow this made me feel very vulnerable. I knew we had faced death as we were tossed about in the small boat, and I also knew that it had exposed a weakness that I never realised I had.

Within a very short time, however, the old bravado had returned, and I was living life to the full as usual. And yet there was now an almost imperceptible awareness that there was a deep aching void in my heart, that the growing display of trophies and the praise of men had failed to fill. I often tried to analyse my growing discontent.

"Surely success in the sporting and enter-tainment world was what every young person craved for," I told myself. Indeed, I was fast approaching a time when I could truly say "I have arrived."But I knew deep down that I wasn't really happy. I was conscious that my apparent enjoyment was a mere facade. This feeling gradually became a burning conviction. I was becoming more and more miserable, and I began to wonder how long I could keep up this false front, and maintain the image I had designed for myself. At some particular moment behind that harbour wall the seed of an impression had been sown in my mind, and now it had germinated.

That impression had something to do with the fleeting character of life, and the vastness of Eternity. It raised such questions as "Is there a God?" It forced me to face the ultimate question, "If there is a Heaven and Hell after death, where am I going?"

Shortly after this narrow escape, a drowning tragedy took place in the harbour of Macduff. The sad incident left indelible impressions on my already-troubled mind. Along with my irresponssible companion already referred to, I found myself in a dance hall across the street from the harbour in the town of Macduff, a short distance from Banff. Against my better judgment, I had accompanied him to a public house in Whitehills, before arriving at the dance. In the middle of the noise and revelry a shout was heard.

"Someone's in the harbour!"

We ran across the street to find a young man leaning against the railing, and I could see that one of his shoes was missing. Between sobs he described what had happened. He and his companion had been indulging in a bit of friendly tomfoolery. In the process his shoe had fallen into the harbour. He remonstrated with his friend who, acting on impulse, said he would retrieve it. The young man dived into the dark water and lost his life as a result — a life abruptly ended, a family plunged in mourning, and a friend who would probably be affected by pangs of remorse all his days, all because of a miserable shoe.

As the searchlight played on the water and the grappling hook was thrown in time and time

again without success, I was convinced that life
was far too precious to waste in this way. I knew
that I was wasting my own life by the way I was
now living, and yet I just didn't know what to do
about it.

To the onlooker I was just a young man without
a serious thought in my head, but in reality my
mind was constantly dwelling on great and vital
questions. These were too deep-rooted to be
dislodged, or even stifled by the hollow laughter
of my fun-loving environment. I began to search
for answers in deep earnest. The first thing I did
was to join the Church of Scotland. The reader
will agree I'm sure that with my background,
such a step was nothing short of remarkable. If
anyone had asked me why I had done such a thing,
I couldn't have given a rational explanation. I
knew I was searching for something, but what it
was I just couldn't say.

Now it isn't my purpose to criticise any
particular church or religious group. Although
my understanding of the Scriptures led me in
later years to break my links with the
denominations, let me make it clear that I have
still the utmost respect for many who are still
linked with them. Indeed, let me be allowed to
state that I know many of them live lives that put
mine to shame, because of their devotedness to
Christ, according to the light they have. Who can
deny that some of the godliest of saints, such as
Robert Murray McCheyne, were linked with the
denominations? Such were totally committed to
winning the lost for Christ. They were without

doubt born-again believers, evangelical in their outlook, and unswerving in their desire to obey God's Word as they understood it. I've no doubt such men occupy some pulpits today. Having said that, however, I must in all honesty state that the minister of the mentioned church was not of this category.

I went along to the vestry for a number of weeks to receive tuition with a view to becoming a member of the church. I was then sprinkled with a little drop of water on my forehead because I had not been christened as a child. I was given a little card with gold lettering which told me that I was now a child of the Kingdom of God, or something to that effect. A group of elders welcomed me as a new member of the church.

In spite of a very busy life, I managed to attend church fairly regularly. I was in real earnest to find the answers to the questions that continually festered in my mind. But I found no satisfactory solution. At first I blamed myself for not being able to understand what the sermons were all about. I really struggled hard to follow the drift of what the minister had to say. But time and time again I was overtaken by sheer boredom. I found myself counting the tubes of the pipe-organ dozens of times to fill in the hour. (I have since learned that my impressions were shared by a large number of the congregation who were glad when the man left the area.) Before long I had become totally disillusioned, and the little card with the gold-gilt lettering gave me no consolation whatsoever. Formal religion had failed to satisfy

the crying needs of my heart. I continued to
search.

# Chapter 11

## HOOKED

I can't remember exactly how I became hooked. No, I hadn't become a drug addict, and smoking and drinking were not a part of my normal lifestyle. I know it happened one Sunday night as we were on our usual round of visiting the local cafes. There was little else to do in those days, and the arrival of a television set in our favourite cafe made it our Mecca for a while. There we drank coffee and marvelled at the new wonder that was to become so commonplace in a very short time. It was outside this cafe that my closest friend George and I became the "victims" of street "fishers". These were young people from the Baptist Church nearby, who combed the streets (and cafes too) inviting young people to an after-church service. This service was geared to meet the needs of young people, they claimed, and everyone was welcome to come without any obligation of any description. I learned later that their method of inviting people off the street was called "street fishing", and it certainly proved to be a fruitful activity in those days.

Among those engaged in the work that night were two young men of my own age group. One had been in my own class at school and I was quite surprised to see him involved in such activity.

since he was, even in my estimation, a very worldly young man. Both of them worked in a local shipyard and it occurred to me that what they were doing required a special type of courage. This fact alone triggered off my curiosity, and without making it too obvious, I found myself listening to what they had to say.

They told me that they had got saved. I smirked but let them continue. Earnestly they related how they had been to a *Billy Graham Crusade* meeting in Inverness, and had heard the Gospel. The preacher had pointed out from the Bible that everyone stood condemned before God, because all had sinned. With joy radiating from their faces they went on to say that it had been pointed out from the Bible that Jesus had taken the sinners' guilt upon Himself, and had suffered and died on the cross for them. Through believing God's Word that he was a sinner and accepting Jesus as his Substitute and Saviour, a man could, without doubt, be saved. They spoke with confidence and yet with sincerity.

"We have done that, and now we know we are saved," they added without any trace of embarrassment.

Now this approach left me with mixed feelings. I was certainly impressed by their courage and fervour, but there was something about this eyeball-to-eyeball type of encounter that frightened me. People were not supposed to invade the personal lives of others in this way, and to "wear your religion on your sleeve" was to my way of thinking extremely distasteful. I wanted a form of religion that could, first of all, answer my deep need, but also remain at the periphery of my life. I didn't want it to impinge upon my private life. In other words, I wanted something that I could keep at a safe distance. After all, I knew quite a number of people who called themselves Christians, and they didn't allow their religion to make any drastic demands on their life-styles. Ministers were trained to do the preaching, and that was what they were paid for. They christened children, married couples and attended to funerals. They were in the front line as far as the public was concerned. The praise and the rebuffs were theirs by choice and the others were merely spectators, watching from a safe distance. I was genuinely puzzled by these two, young, non-academic, shipyard workers, as they talked so easily about their new-found faith, and I wondered what they were really up to.

"What you need, Charles, is not religion; it's Christ. You need a new relationship with God. You need to make a new start with God." They were almost waxing eloquent as they took turns to speak to me. "You see," they continued, "only a real, vital, lasting relationship with God can really meet your need."

Although these two young men knew me fairly well, they could not have imagined the impact of such comments on my inner being. I had virtually written off religion in my search for the answers to the great enigma of existence. I had never heard of the necessity of being saved. In fact most of the terms used by the youthful preachers that night were strange to my ear, but I didn't want to show my ignorance by asking what they really meant. In any case their most potent argument wasn't so much in what they had to say that night, but the sheer joy that animated them, as they tried to share with me something that was obviously of ultimate importance to them.

"What about coming down to our Youth Fellowship?" they asked, sensing my interest.

George, my companion, had been standing nearby listening to the conversation. Looking at him I asked, "Well George, what do you think?"

"I'm game, if you are," he shrugged.

As we made our way down to the little hall at the rear of the main Baptist Church building I could not help reflecting that George and I were probably the most unusual "fish" that had ever been hooked by those young "fishers of men". For several years we had been inseparable chums. We went everywhere together, and the accounts of our escapades could fill a book themselves. He was a born comedian and there was never a dull moment in his company. My mind went to the time when we had gone on holiday to Fleetwood together. We had exhausted all that the Golden Mile had to offer and things were becoming a bit stale. Jimmie, my oldest brother, happened to come in from a fishing-trip and he noticed that we were bored.

"Like to come with the boys tonight?" he asked, with a suspicious grin on his face. "We're going pub-crawling tonight. Some of my mates are home and we are going to have a great time."

Neither of us knew what was meant by pub-crawling, but we sensed a hint of a challenge in his invitation and we felt we couldn't refuse.

"Sure we'll go," we chorused, little knowing what we were letting ourselves in for. For one thing both of us were too interested in our own particular sport to indulge in drinking sprees (George was a footballer of no mean ability). Only on very rare occasions, such as the annual Hogmanay celebrations would either of us be induced to drink alcohol. I personally hated the taste of the stuff, but like many another young person, I just went along with the crowd to be sociable.

The taxi drew up at the door and we all piled in. The driver would be our chauffeur for the rest of the night. He was to get his full share of the alcoholic beverages in the various public-houses and night-clubs we were to visit, and it was a source of wonder to me that he was able to stand at all, far less drive a taxi, by the time the night was over.

At the first pub, about six of us gathered in a side room and George and I exchanged looks as we heard the plans for the evening being discussed. We stared, completely mesmerised, as they threw a pile of five and ten pound notes on to the table to form a kitty, to pay for the evening's entertainment. We fumbled in our pockets and both of us sheepishly slipped a ten shilling note into the pile. We hoped they wouldn't notice our rather pathetic contribution, but alas, it wasn't to be.

Amidst gales of laughter, my brother bellowed,

"We're alright tonight lads, we've got the last of the big spenders with us." We squirmed and tried to protest that we had spent all our money in Blackpool.

It began to dawn on me that we had been brought along to provide a source of entertainment for those drink-hardened, young trawlfishermen. I made a mental note that they were not going to get fun at my expense. The first round of drinks was consumed. I struggled to drink the "rum and pep" they had given me without screwing up my face in complete revulsion. I managed to drain my glass of this petrol-like substance without flinching, and attempted to put on a show of bravado. But the night's drinking orgy had just begun. The floor was beginning to come up to meet me as I followed the others out of that room to embark on the craziest night I have ever spent in my life.

Our driver knew the twilight-zone area very well. From one club we went to another and each time I was getting dizzier and dizzier. The more we staggered the more our companions seemed to enjoy themselves. At one particular club, a man all made up with lipstick and paint tried to engage us in conversation. My brother thought this very hilarious. What with blurred speech and a heavy Scottish accent, we found conversation just about impossible. It was just as well, for we had never even heard of, far less seen, a male homosexual before. Our naive attitudes were just ready to be exploited by my brother and his friends. After finally telling this strange individual to "Get lost" he turned to my chum George, who was beginning to become extremely jovial by now.

"I believe you're quite a good singer George. What about a good old-fashioned Scottish song?"

George required no more prompting, and from then on we were entertained to the strains of a current popular Scottish song, "The Northern Lights of Old Aberdeen". From the point of view of entertainment value, this was quite acceptable in the smaller clubs, but the problem was we couldn't get him stopped. In the first few clubs no permission was required from the management.

"Away you go then, George," from my brother, backed up with a wink to his pals, was all the motivation Buckie's answer to Robert Wilson required. In fact he usually got a resounding cheer from the other customers and sometimes a request for "more".

All went well until we found ourselves staggering into a huge, palatial hotel. As far as my blurred memory serves me, I can recall a vast carpeted lounge with tables all round. The floor was raised every now and then leading to an area at the rear where a small orchestra was playing soft music under coloured lights. An immaculate conductor was leading this small group, the various colours reflecting on his spotless white dinner-jacket. I immediately felt out of place in this extremely high-brow nightspot. I was reflecting on the possible reasons for this place being included in our nocturnal trek, when I was horrified to see my erstwhile singer-friend scrambling up the steps towards the orchestra. Unnoticed, he finally reached the top landing and lurched towards the microphone.

"I'm fae Scotland and I'm gan tae sing tae ye 'The Northern Lights of Old Aberdeen'." The words seemed so incongruous as a deathly hush filled the lounge. The soft music stopped abruptly and the conductor turned to glare at the one who had dared to invade the sanctity of his rostrum. Beside himself with rage, he hurled himself upon the inebriate frame of our Scottish songster. Holding firmly on to the microphone, George put up a valiant struggle. Occasional snippets of conversation were blurted through the microphone.

"Look, mate, I'm fae Scotland," came through loud and clear several times but this seemingly impregnable argument was finally destroyed by a tirade of language, interlaced with a few curses for emphasis, from the conductor, "I don't care if you come from Ireland, you are certainly not going to sing here." After a few reinforcements were sent in, a rather sulky George was firmly deposited beside our group at the table.

Apart from a potentially serious argument in another nightclub over the taxi-driver drinking George's whisky when he was up singing, I can remember nothing at all until I woke up with a severe headache next morning. George had the last laugh on me, because he was able to describe clearly my unconscious figure being carried from the taxi into my mother's house, whilst he could have carried on all night.

And here we were, two young men who, to the onlooker, apparently had never entertained a serious thought in their whole lives, going to a religious meeting — a course of action that was to affect our whole destiny.

Perhaps this isn't so strange after all. Perhaps we all tend to poke fun at ultimate realities such as death and Hell. We can so easily put on a kind of lighthearted camouflage and try to give the impression that we couldn't care less. Our case at least shows that outward bravado and facetious behaviour can be very misleading. Deep down, whilst never admitting it, we were seriously concerned about spiritual and eternal matters.

I don't know what I expected at this particular meeting, but what immediately struck me was the warmth of the welcome received, and the obvious joy that everyone seemed to possess.

"Glad to see you, boys," said the white-haired "old man" at the door. He pumped our hands in welcome as if we were long-lost friends. It was Mr. Barr, the minister. Although he looked much older, he must have been still in his thirties then. He certainly wasn't long in proving to me that he had a dynamic personality, and knew how to motivate young people. But he had a back seat that night, for this was the *Christian Endeavour* meeting run by the young people themselves. A time of chorus singing was followed by a time of prayer. Some young people then gave their testimonies, describing how the Lord Jesus had saved them and was keeping them day by day. It was all very informal and there was no attempt to "buttonhole" anyone. I left that meeting feeling that I was at last on the right road. Our "Street Fishers" had us hooked, but as every fisher will know, it is one thing to have a fish on the hook, but it is far more important to land that fish. But they had learned the art of landing the fish well. In later years I was to learn the art where it alone can be learned — at the feet of the One who said "Come ye after Me and I will make you to become fishers of men." In any case they kept a tight hold of the line, inviting us to meetings, inviting us to the homes of those given to hospitality, and no doubt praying for us that we would yield our lives to Christ.

What impressed me perhaps more than anything else, was the fact that these young men and women not only witnessed for Christ, but they lived Christ. It wasn't just a Sunday-Only Christianity with them. They didn't have a set pattern of behaviour on a Sunday and a different set during the week. Yet there was no eccentricity or affectation. Whilst they all had a genuine passion for lost souls, I can never recall a single incident when I was embarrassed by an over zealous soul-winner. Every activity was the overflow of warm Christian love and fellowship.

I soon learned some of the choruses and hymns which were firm favourites at that time, due to the campaigns organised by Billy Graham just prior to this. "Blessed Assurance Jesus is Mine", and "To God be the Glory Great Things He Hath Done" became my own particular favourites. Very slowly my basically shy, undemonstrative nature, faded into the background, and, soon George and I were the loudest singers of them all. But we were still not saved. The fish had not yet been landed.

We found ourselves attending the Gospel Service every Sunday evening in the main church building. Mr. Barr preached a powerful Gospel message every week. He made the way of salvation clear and plain in a refreshing, vigorous manner. He made it clear that salvation was not a matter of what the sinner had done, or had not done — it was entirely a matter of what Christ had done on the sinner's behalf on the Cross of Calvary. He fearlessly heralded forth the solemn message that unless a man be born again, all his own righteousness, respectability and religion, would lead him down the slippery slopes to a lost Eternity in Hell. He made sure that everyone in the congregation understood that it was the Blood of Jesus Christ alone that cleansed the sinner from all sin. In short he clearly taught the three R's — Man's Ruin, God's Remedy and Man's Responsibility.

Sometimes he let some of the young people take over the pulpit and in this way helped them to develop their preaching gifts. As a result of this encouragement, a number of young men rapidly grew in spiritual stature. As an indication of the calibre of the young men attending the Baptist Church at that time, it is interesting to note that no less than three of them entered the ministry shortly afterwards, whilst another later became a full-time evangelist within brethren circles.

Sometimes itinerant preachers were given the opportunity to preach at the Gospel Service and at the Christian Endeavour meeting. Occasionally a guest speaker would come from another evangelical church in the town. One delightful character spoke in broad Scots. His name was Johnnie Cowie and he was linked with the Salvation Army.

Although strong impressions were being made on my mind as I listened to the preaching of the Word of God, it seemed that they were lost to a certain extent during the hectic activities of the week. This period of my life was marked by alternate fits of genuine concern — even remorse — and also thoughtless frivolity. This ambivalence I find hard to explain. I was being pulled in opposite directions. I realised later that Satan was doing his utmost to drag me away from God. But at that time Satan was nothing more than a mere figment of the imagination as far as I was concerned. As I listened to the young Christians giving their testimonies, (invariably introduced by the words "I was brought up in a Christian home") I felt I would have done anything or given everything I had, to possess the peace and the assurance they so obviously enjoyed. And yet during the week there were times when I counted the cost, and dreaded what my workmates would say if I became a Christian and gave up my old way of life. I felt that I just wouldn't be able to tolerate any scoffing, and in any case I wasn't altogether sure that I wanted to give up my sporting and danceband activities.

This confused state of mind continued throughout the winter of 1955. The chorus-singing no
longer lifted my spirit as it once did, but rather
left me more depressed than ever. I realised that I
had been singing about matters outwith my own
experience. I felt that I had no right to sing such
words as "I have decided to follow Jesus, No
turning back, no turning back". I knew deep
down in my heart that I was putting the world
before me and the cross behind me and not the
reverse, as I had often sung so lustily. Even an
occasional feeling of bitterness crept into my
mind as I pondered the possibility that being
"brought up in a Christian home" was part of a
"deal" that left me out in the cold.

The afternoon sun had a hint of warmth as I
cycled through the woods on my way to
Fochabers. Patches of snow lay here and there
among the conifer trees, proving that Winter was
by no means over. I had travelled this road a few
times since Buckie Boxing Club had folded up. I
had become a member of the Fochaber's Club and
had trained with my new clubmates on regular
occasions. After training sessions, I would run the
six miles home to Buckie alone. At night this part
of the journey could be a bit unnerving, I mused,
as I gazed at the heavily-wooded landscape. I had
to be at Mr. Allison's, our trainer, for a light tea.
Then it was off to The North East of Scotland
Amateur Boxing Championship tournament in
the Music Hall, Aberdeen. I had taken the
afternoon off my work in order to be in Fochabers

in time.

The journey to Aberdeen in the special bus didn't seem to take us long. The local boxers had their own retinue of vociferous supporters and they were in very high spirits. Most of the people were strangers to me and I felt very much alone. I missed my old friend George, and as the language wasn't always desirable, I began to feel that I didn't fit into this kind of company.

The Music Hall was packed to capacity when we arrived. The atmosphere was tense with excitement. As usual, the tobacco smoke whirled under the bright lights above the boxing-ring. The sight of a boxing ring always sent the adrenaline flowing through my bloodstream, and this occasion was no different. There was the added excitement of boxing before television cameras, and it was only after the event that we were told that the equipment wasn't fitted up in time.

"Keep your guard up and everything will be O.K. Don't let him force you into a slugging match. Keep that straight left going and then a few solid left-right combinations upstairs and downstairs." Mr. Allison was giving me a few last instructions before I boxed in the final which would decide who would be the North East of Scotland Lightweight Champion. Earlier on in the evening my opponent and I had won the semi-final bouts. My opponent had been from one of the Aberdeen clubs and had a large following of supporters. Our tiny group from Fochabers was drowned out completely and I felt so lonely that I

went out to sit in the night air on a bench a few
yards down Union Street. It was good to get out of
the smoky atmosphere for a while. As the traffic
passed by, I was alone with my thoughts. I was
unhappy. Deep down in my heart there was an
empty void that had not been filled as yet. As I
headed back to the hall I knew I had lost the will
to fight.

"Seconds out, first round." The piercing note of
the bell heralded the commencement of the bout.
The resin tray was whipped away and Mr. Allison
was outside of the ring.

I will refrain from dwelling too closely on the
details of the bout. Suffice it to say that my
opponent was an extremely powerful puncher,
but lacked boxing skill. Contrary to Mr. Allison's
instructions, however, I did allow myself to be
involved in a brawl. Strangely enough, I knew I
was doing the wrong thing. Mentally I knew that
boxing skill was the only successful way to tackle
this type of boxer. And yet I seemed to be unable
to carry out this approach in practice. Throwing
overboard all the experience of several years, I
swung toe to toe with this streetfighter type of
boxer. Of course the crowd loved every moment of
it. In fact I was amazed to hear the partisan
crowd jeer at the decision which gave the title to
the Aberdonian. I left the ring to a thunderous
applause. My opponent came to my dressing-
room later to express his appreciation for the
great fight I had put up. I felt it was a very poor
performance on my part, and I was glad to learn
that it had not been televised as had been

expected.

I felt sorry for Mr. Allison. He thought it was a dreadful decision and said so in no uncertain terms. He probably sensed how I felt and made no comment about a performance totally out of character with my ability. Having piled my bicycle into his landrover, he drove me home to Buckie. He tried to encourage me by saying that I was sure to be included in the team going to some other championships in the south of Scotland. I was hardly listening to him. Deep down I knew that I would not be there. As we turned down the last mile into Buckie around midnight, I somehow sensed that my life was fast approaching a crisis point.

# Chapter 12

## THE FISH LANDED

Mr. Heatherington and Mr. Dukelow had a distinctive style of preaching. It was my first taste of the Irish presentation of the Gospel. They introduced us to another three R's - Ruin by the Fall; Regeneration by the Spirit and Redemption by the Blood. They were attached to the Faith Mission and had come to conduct Gospel meetings in the bowling-green pavilion in the little village of Findochty, a couple of miles from Buckie. They were working very closely with the Buckie Baptist Church and other evangelical groups in the area. As a result, their meetings were well attended. There was a feeling of expectation for the believers had been praying hard for blessing. There was unity and a oneness of purpose as night after night the message was told forth. One night the awful tragedy of dying without Christ and landing in the Lake of Fire without Christ would form the theme of the message, and the next the wonderful love of God. Occasionally someone would sing a solo. On one occasion all the fishermen in the audience were told to come to the front to sing "Will Your Anchor Hold In The Storms of Life?" The meetings were very informal and yet there was a sense of reverence at the same time.

"Mr. Cowie will sing a lovely hymn that tells us of God's love. Most of you will know it — 'Love Lifted Me'." The clear tenor voice of Mr. Cowie filled the pavilion.

"I was sinking deep in sin,
Sinking to rise no more,
Overwhelmed by guilt within,
Mercy I did implore,
Then the Master of the sea,
Heard my despairing cry,
Christ my Saviour lifted me,
Now safe am I."

All at once the whole congregation broke in with the chorus —

"Love lifted me, love lifted me,
When no one but Christ could help,
Love lifted me."

I felt the tear run down my cheek. These people could sing with such joy. They just couldn't restrain themselves from singing the chorus. The love of God had indeed lifted them from the depths of sin. I felt the most miserable creature that had ever lived. Oh! if only I could sincerely sing these words. George, my partner in so many foolish escapades, was singing them, for in the home of this same Mr. Cowie, he had yielded his life to Christ. With a strong voice he was singing above them all. I wiped away the tear and listened to the next verse.

"Souls in danger look above,
Jesus completely saves,
He will lift you by His love,
Out of the angry waves,
He's the Master of the sea,
Billows His will obey,
He your Saviour wants to be,
Be saved today."

Again my eyes swam with tears as everyone, apart from myself, joined in the chorus. The last verse seemed to open the flood-gates of my heart completely as the tears came freely.

"When the waves of sorrow roll,
When I am in distress,
Jesus takes my hand in His,
Ever He loves to bless,
He will every fear dispel,
Satisfy every need,
All who heed His loving call,
Find rest indeed."

The rapturous, spontaneous singing of the words, "Love Lifted Me" must have been heard in every corner of Findochty. Every word had been like an arrow of conviction in my heart. I knew my tears were not the product of mere, shallow, sentimental emotion. I had felt as if this hymn had been specially written for me. More than anything else in the whole world, I wished I had been able to have sung from experience that God's love had lifted me from the sea of sin. But I left that meeting still on the Broad Road to Hell. It seemed as if Satan wasn't going to give up this fish without a struggle.

Those who suffer from psoriasis will know how quickly it can spread over the whole body. I knew that it was becoming worse, and the specialist was beginning to use the term a chronic case. Every day, morning and evening, I had to apply the coaltar treatment. With the condition so extensive it meant that most of my body had to be treated with the ointment. Working outside on a building-site during the winter can be very cold at the best of times. One can imagine how cold I was with my body literally covered with this clammy substance. My scalp was in such a mess of scaly patches that I had to get a workmate to give me a haircut, because I obviously couldn't go to any of our local hairdressers. Instead of getting better, I was becoming decidedly worse. The patches were becoming larger and joining with other patches to completely cover some sections of my body. The irritation was becoming unbearable and life was becoming a nightmare. Many a night I would call on God to take me away from this existence, and then I would remember that I wasn't saved and would land in the eternal misery of Hell and the Lake of Fire. On several occasions I contemplated suicide. After washing the scales off my body at night in my bedroom, I would apply the tar. By this time my whole body seemed to be on fire. I tried to hide my suffering from my old Grannie, and I would always put on the tar myself. It was after one of those evening sessions that I turned on the gas-tap and lay back in the chair. I was in such a mess that I couldn't bear to look at myself in the mirror. Fluid had been gathering in my legs and I could poke my fingers into the flesh for about an inch without any feeling. As the minutes ticked away I had the most wonderful sensation of relief. In a few minutes I would be rid of this heart-breaking affliction. I would just sleep away ......

"That's a fine way to treat your old Grannie isn't it?" What gave birth to the thought I'll never know. What I do know is that it somehow registered in my befuddled brain. A kind of mental picture floated before my mind's eye, showing my Grannie in a terrible state of distress looking down at my lifeless form. No, after all her kindness to me I just couldn't do this to her. My hand groped for the tap at the side of the mantelshelf and I switched it off. I sat for a long time just staring into the darkness. It slowly began to dawn on me that, in all probability, the gas would have seeped through the house and ushered my old Grannie into a Christless Eternity. And I would have entered the presence of a Holy God still unsaved, to be finally banished from His presence into the Lake of Fire forever.

"You just can't go on like this, you'll have to go into the hospital for proper treatment." The doctor was resolute and completely ignored my protests. I had always dreaded going into the hospital, because I wanted as few people to know that I had the disease as possible. As there were few traces of it on my face, I was able to conceal my secret well. Few people were aware of the real nature or extent of my affliction. I had always felt extremely sorry for women sufferers who obviously couldn't conceal it so well as men.

The necessary arrangements were quickly made. I brushed aside all offers of transport and made my way up to our local hospital at the appointed time. I slowly dragged my painful legs across the playing-field that provided a short cut, wishing with every step that I hadn't been so stubborn about the offered lifts. It seemed incredible that I had been in the peak of physical condition only a few weeks before, and here I was shuffling along like an old man.

That morning I had reached the lowest depths of despair. The water had turned my body into a stinging mass of raw flesh. Almost demented with unrelenting pain, I had seized a Bible from a shelf and thrown it across the floor as an animal-like roar of defiance came to my throat. Dredged up from the dark depths of my baser instincts there poured forth from my lips, words of the vilest nature. Revolt against life itself surged through my heart like a raging torrent, finally giving way to an emotional climax of unspeakable despair. I was trapped and knew it. I didn't want to live, but I knew also that death did not hold the answer.

The sun suddenly broke free from a cloud as I passed the cemetery that adjoins the hospital grounds. It was the first week in April and the golden daffodils lining the driveway made me forget my misery for a moment. From the dark, cold death of winter they had emerged to delight us with their beauty. I lingered as long as I could, watching them gently gyrating in the soft breeze, and then I headed for the hospital entrance nearby.

"What on earth's this? Was there a snowstorm in here last night?" It was the morning cleaner. Her surprised tone made it obvious that she had never encountered a psoriasis patient in the ward before. I squirmed with embarrassment at the large amount of scales that lay almost accusingly all over the polished floor. The coaltar bath I had the night before had loosened the scales and the endless itching throughout the night had deposited them, indeed like snowflakes, on to the floor. "If only I had been sent to the Aberdeen Hospital," I sighed inwardly, for I felt so conspicuous and vulnerable in a hospital where everyone knew me. I realised later, of course, that the staff were genuinely concerned about me, and had no desire to hurt my feelings.

After a few days of ultra-violet lamp treatment, coaltar baths and coaltar ointment applications, I began to feel a lot better. The dreadful itch subsided as did the swelling in my legs. I began to take an interest in my fellow patients. They were all what was termed then, "geriatric patients". One or two groaned all night long and kept me awake. Some had a rare sense of humour that advanced years and mental and physical weakness had failed to destroy. Sometimes tempers flared and threats were hurled across the ward at each other. When one considered that they couldn't get out of bed, far less carry out the threats, the ludicrous cameraderie was tinged with sadness. These were once strong, working men, but now they were reduced to total helplessness.

One beautiful morning the windows were opened to let in the spring air. Not a sound could be heard apart from the mating birds singing their love-songs. Then I heard it. The faint cry of a newborn baby coming from the maternity wing close by. How appropriate it seemed at that magic moment, when one was drinking in the wonder of a peaceful Spring morning. Everything was bursting into life after a cold, cruel winter, and here was a tiny babe contributing to the amazing pattern.

A long groan came from the corner of the room. It came from the patient at the far corner of the ward who always kept his head covered with the sheets. The marvels of nature had long lost their appeal to him. He was groaning out his last few days of existence on earth. I began to think along a more sombre line again. What was the point of it all? Why birth? Why has this child been born only to become in a few years' time like this poor suffering creature in the corner — a pleasure to no one, least of all to himself? That same afternoon I was stretching my legs by walking along the corridor. As I paused to look out of the window, I spotted the funeral cortege winding its way up the driveway into the cemetery. Again I brooded over the purpose of life. Why was that child born? Why is that poor senile man suffering? Why has this person died? There just didn't seem to be any sense in it at all. Here within a few hundred square metres was a tiny microcosm of human existence — birth, suffering and death.

It was the 24th April. I had made rapid progress physically. The scales had stopped reforming and faint, red patches were all that could be seen on my body. It was wonderful to get a good night's sleep. My companion George had been up the previous day with the trophy that I had won in Aberdeen as the runner-up. It had arrived when I was in hospital. The silver figure in the boxing stance was placed on my locker. My mind was on other things, however. When I was wakened very early in the morning as is the normal custom in hospitals, my thoughts were still dwelling on those things. I would be going home later that day. I would be going back to my old way of life. The hectic round of activities would soon drive any serious thoughts from my mind. I had regained my health, and a joy of living — on a mere physical plane, was beginning to dominate my attitude. A battle was raging inside once again. Somehow I realised that I had been quietly pondering things in the calm surroundings of the hospital. Somehow I realised that I had approached the hour of decision — it was now or never. For some unknown reason I was convinced that if I walked out of that hospital unsaved, I would never be saved.

I quietly slipped into the little ward which was next to the one I had been in for the last fortnight. Apart from a little organ the place was empty.

The organ was used each Sunday evening by a group from one of the local churches. It was carried from ward to ward during the course of the visit. I sat down on the stool and thumbed through the *Billy Graham Song Book* lying on the organ. Soon my eyes were reading the words of the hymn, "Love Lifted Me". The evening in the bowling-green pavilion in Findochty came back to me with tremendous force. I read it once, then I read it again very slowly, drinking in every word. It began to dawn on me that God had brought me away from the hustle and bustle of life to this hospital, in order that He might speak to me alone. I gradually thought of all that I had heard about God and His love. I began to see so clearly that God loved me as an individual. I could see that I was sinking deep in sin, but I realised that God had done everything possible in order to save me from the punishment my sins so rightly deserved. I realised that I had to look above, away from self, to the One Who could completely save — the One Who could lift and liberate me from the awful bondage of sin. Without any human agency to guide me, I there and then yielded my life, body and soul and spirit, to the Lord Jesus Christ for time and eternity.

There were no sensational feelings. I didn't hear any angelic voices burst forth into song. But that made no difference for one's salvation does not depend on feelings — it depends upon the unchanging Word of God. Up until that moment I had acquiesced in a mental way with all that the preachers had said, but now I was resting without reserve on the finished work of the Lord Jesus on the Cross of Calvary. I firmly believed that "My sins deserved eternal death, but Jesus died for me". God had said it, I believed it, and that was enough for me. The matter was settled as far as I was concerned. A Divine Power had in mercy lifted the heavy portcullis from my soul and the light of God's wonderful love streamed in. From the dark lonely shadows of despair, I stepped by faith into the sunlight of a brand new, abundant life in Christ. Whilst not depending on feelings, the assurance that I was saved brought overwhelming joy into my heart. I had at last found what I had been searching for so long — the "peace of God that passeth all understanding". I could now sing from my heart the hymn:

"Just as I am, Thy love unknown,
Has broken every barrier down,
Now to be Thine, yea Thine alone,
Oh Lamb of God I come, I come."

Later that day I left hospital and to me there was a beauty in everything I saw. There was a spring in my step and a new song in my mouth, and yes, it was "Love Lifted Me". Along that same road I had shuffled a fortnight earlier, the most miserable wretch upon the face of the earth. Now I was returning with a "Joy unspeakable and full of Glory". I was a new person altogether. I had been born-again. I had made a new start with God. The fish was safely landed at last.

"Grannie," I said, as we were about to have our

tea, "I want to do something that we have never done here before." I couldn't bring myself to look into her face as I bowed my head, so I don't know what kind of expression she had. I quietly, and briefly thanked the Lord for His kindness in providing the meal that was set before us. She didn't make any comment about our new innovation, but she must have sensed that a change had taken place in my life. The giving of thanks for our meals became a standard practice with us from then on.

Although a distinct change had taken place in my life, I didn't throw overboard my interest in boxing right away. Within a few weeks I was in the ring again. The period in the hospital had sapped my energy and I never got my "second wind" at all during the bout. As a result I was gasping for air all the time, and, although I won the bout, I felt that I had been humiliated by a novice before a home crowd. I trained hard for the return bout and there was no doubt about the decision. That was the last occasion, however, that I entered a boxing ring. The pleasure of victory and the excitement of the occasion had left me. I had been daily enjoying the truth of the chorus "Turn your eyes upon Jesus, look full in His wonderful face, and the things of the earth will grow strangely dim, in the light of His Glory and Grace." I had discovered that only the God Who made the heart can really satisfy it. "The joys of earth can never fill, the heart that once has known Thy love." Every born-again believer will testify that this is so.

# Chapter 13

## "MY GRACE ..."

Grannie was now almost eighty years of age, and was still mending nets in the same old, squalid conditions already referred to. Most of her meagre earnings went towards paying the interest on the loan that had been received many years earlier. The loan itself, two hundred pounds, had remained unchanged since the day it had been taken out, and as far as Grannie was concerned, it would just have to remain unpaid.

But now the Lord Jesus was a welcome Guest in that poverty-stricken home, and what a difference that made. Every evening the Bible was opened, and a suitable portion of Scripture was read aloud to Grannie before retiring for the night. How earnestly I prayed in private for her conversion. The thought that she was tottering on the very brink of damnation, drove me to my knees in supplication. Most Christians will agree that those nearest to us by the ties of nature are usually the most difficult to speak to about eternal matters. Sometimes I tried to broach the subject of her position before a holy, sin-hating God, but I found myself tongue-tied and selfconscious. I took comfort, however, in the fact that she never once protested about my short readings of the Holy Scriptures. This amazed me in the light of her past inveterate hostility towards anything of a religious nature. To my great surprise, she once quoted a considerable portion of John's Gospel Chapter 14, after I had started to read at the first verse.

"Learned that at the Sunday School," was all she said with a faint smile of satisfaction. This was a tremendous source of encouragement to me. Here was a precious portion of God's Word, memorised in childhood days, now being resurrected. The hardships and disappointments of life had failed to eradicate from her heart the good seed of the Word of God. The seed had been planted many decades earlier, and I fervently prayed that God would cause it to germinate in her heart before it was forever too late. Sometimes I brought home some mature soul-winner so that a discreet word about the importance of salvation could be passed on to Grannie during our chat around the fireside. Sometimes she quickly changed the topic of conversation or pretended she didn't hear. It seemed to me that she was too set in her ways to change.

Grannie occasionally dropped the hint that I should be thinking of "settlin' doon", as she put it. She meant of course that I should be looking about for a wife. No doubt she realised that she wouldn't be around for very long, and she therefore wanted to see me settled down to married life before she departed from the scene. But that was easier said than done. I wasn't the demonstrative type and my childhood experiences had left certain psychological scars that made it almost impossible for me to express my most intimate feelings. It was basically the fear of being rejected that forced me to shrink from risking an attempt to express my affection for another. This very real, haunting fear, was sometimes hidden behind a show of bravado, or even downright rudeness. This fear of rejection was without a doubt a carry over from the insecurity, the disharmony and the cruel rejection experienced during my most impressionable years. (On a non-intimate level, I had no trouble of course, in relating to other people.)

Because of these "hang-ups", plus the fact that I had suffered, and was still suffering, from recurring attacks of psoriasis, I realised that my chances of getting a life-partner were extremely remote. I was realistic enough to know that I was a very risky proposition in any girl's estimation. In fact, at one point I had resolved myself to what I considered to be the inevitable — the life of a bachelor. But as it happened, there was one girl who was prepared to take the risk, and I will be eternally grateful to God for bringing her into my life.

Grace lived at the end of the street, and was perfectly aware about my dubious background. Her parents were Christians and were members of what was known in the town as "open" brethren. She herself had recently accepted the Lord Jesus as her Saviour. I worked alongside her brother in a building-squad and he brought the news to her that I was more than a little interested in her. He brought back her response, to the effect that she considered the matter a huge joke. I had prepared myself for such a response, so it wasn't altogether unexpected. I simply left the matter with the Lord and was content to live my life as a bachelor, if that was His will for me.

"She's going to the Sunday School picnic tomorrow, but she'll see you afterwards." Frank, her brother, was the speaker, and I think he was more surprised than I was that his only sister was prepared to accept a date with a virtual nobody. As we worked together that day, I was continually subjected to his good-natured banter. (Frank later became a full-time evangelist in the North of Scotland.)

Grace was only sixteen and I was twenty-one. I had known her since childhood, and had watched her grow up into a fine young woman with an infectious smile and a warm personality. I felt awkward as I walked with her around the country-side that lovely summer's evening. She soon put me at ease, however, and the warmth of her gentle nature impressed me more and more as the evening passed. Her knowledge of the Bible was far superior to mine, and, within my heart, I praised the Lord that I had indeed found a virtuous woman whose "price is far above rubies". With the Lord's help and the support of Grace, I knew I could face anything that the future held in store for me.

I soon discovered that it wasn't an easy thing to live the Christian life in a rough squad of working men. Their language and filthy jokes jarred me as never before. I was of no interest to them since giving up the boxing. In fact they began to resent my company. One day as I was heading for the hut where we had our lunch, I spotted some tools lying scattered about in the mud, and I realised that they were mine.

"Get out of here and stay out!" It was the voice of the foreman in charge of the building contract.

"No, we don't want the likes of you in here!" Someone else spoke from the dark corner of the hut, followed by a guffaw of laughter. It was winter and the hut afforded us with the only shelter available. The men had taken exception to my quiet reading of my Bible during the lunchbreak, and now I was ordered out altogether. I quietly gathered my tools together, took my lunch-pack from the hut, and without saying a word, went to the galvanised portable shelter that we used for transportation. We sat inside this going to and from our work on the back of a lorry. It had no door and gave very little protection from the cold. There I sat alone, eating my sandwiches and reading my Bible. And yet I was not alone, for I enjoyed the Presence of the One Whom the world cast out — even the Lord Himself. For many weeks the draughty structure was my daily trysting place with God.

On another occasion I was "sent to Coventry". For weeks on end I was totally ignored by the squad. With great difficulty I struggled to keep my temper and get on with the work at hand. I couldn't refrain from singing and gradually they saw that I had an inner joy that their vindictiveness just couldn't destroy. I never complained to my boss or showed any animosity. I was a follower of One Who "When He was reviled, he reviled not again; when He suffered, He threatened not."

My singing of choruses and hymns seemed to irritate some of them, (although I didn't try to annoy them). One day I was working at the top of a new house and was giving vent to the joy in my heart.

"Oh give us a break," somebody shouted from the other end of the building. I smiled and just carried on.

All at once my head exploded. "I'll shut him up!" I heard the voice of one of my fellow-workers. I could see nothing but stars and flashes. Then another blow came and I blindly threw myself on to the rafters as my legs buckled. I held on tightly to prevent myself from falling down on to the joists below. The man was a bitter Roman Catholic and he had expressed his implacable hatred on a number of occasions. Now he had actually struck me over the head with a brick hammer. The hammer is quite light and I had a cloth working cap on, but nevertheless a full blow on the head in such a fit of frenzy could have been fatal. I don't know what happened in the moments that followed. I can only assume that someone restrained him, or he realised the implication of what he had done. I blacked out for a minute or two and came to with blurred vision and a splitting headache.

Only God's grace prevented me from retaliating

after the first blow. Every fibre in my body screamed for retaliation against the fanatical tormentor, but a greater Power within enabled me to put up no resistance whatsoever.

Of course I felt keenly the cruel, causeless attitude of my colleagues. But as I would pour out my complaints to Grace I found in her one who could really understand and sympathise. Time and again she would point out the Scriptural attitude that the Christian should adopt when faced with reproach.

That summer, George and I went with Mr.Barr and a group of young people to the seaside town of Ayr. During that visit we got to know quite a number of fine young Christians from various parts of the country. We were based in the Baptist Church and I shall never forget Mr.McKendrick the minister. During the fellowship meetings in the evenings we were invited to bombard him with texts from the Bible, and he answered by giving the chapter and verse we had quoted. He obviously had a remarkable, factual knowledge of the Scriptures.

Our days were fully occupied with beachwork, speaking to the children of holidaymakers. I shall never forget one particular evening as the sun slowly slipped behind the Ailsa Craig. A hush had fallen on the little knots of visitors as they drank in the beauty of the scene. All the young people were sitting along the concrete wall, wrapt in a silence that almost bordered on worship. Sensing the mood of the moment, I clipped on my saxophone and started to play, "The Lord's My

Shepherd", to the tune, "Crimond". By the second verse everyone had joined in. As the last rays of the sun played against a passing patch of cloud, the lovely words filled the evening air:

"Goodness and mercy all my life,
Shall surely follow me,
And in God's house forevermore,
My dwelling place shall be."

One felt at the very gate of Heaven, and I have no doubt that quite a few of those present locked those golden moments inside the casket of memory, to be enjoyed in future days. Almost twenty years later, a Christian lady told me personally that her daughter, who was dying with cancer, made reference to those same fleeting moments. I wasn't really surprised to know that, like myself, she had felt so close to God, and the experience had left indelible impressions on her heart.

This was my first real taste of Christian fellowship. At night there were some good-natured, although noisy, discussions about doctrinal issues. Some of those present represented different denominations, and I didn't know enough about the Bible to offer even the slightest contribution. I did wonder now and then why there should be so many different groups of Christians. It seemed to be so wonderful to be together as we were. It was beyond question that we would all be together in Heaven. I couldn't understand it, so I just gave up trying.

Although I had never become an official member of the Baptist Church, I was in full sympathy with its teachings. I was very happy there, and there was no pressure brought to bear on me to become an official member. As I continued to read my Bible, however, I began to discover that the chorus singing and the other activities weren't satisfying my growing spiritual thirst. As I was invited by Grace to the homes of believers linked with brethren, I soon realised that my spiritual life was beginning to develop as we discussed the Scriptures together. I was immediately impressed by their love for, and knowledge of, the Living Word. I had always treated such people who met in the Gospel Hall with the utmost suspicion. During those social visits with Grace, I realised that many of the allegations laid against them were totally groundless. Whilst not without failure, some of the dear saints who lavished their kindness upon me at this time are without a doubt, "The salt of the earth". Davy and Peggy came into this category. When I visited their home they treated me like a son of their own. They took me not only into their home, but also into their hearts.

During such visits, I continually asked questions of a spiritual nature. Invariably our conversation developed into the form of a Bible reading. Davy had been saved in later life, but his general knowledge of spiritual matters made me feel that I was merely paddling in the shallow pools, when beyond lay the great ocean of Divine revelation waiting to be discovered experimentally. Sometimes I tried to provoke them into an argument, but both Davy and Peggy always managed to take the sting out of my reasonings.

"But why adopt this 'holier than thou — we are the people' attitude?" I would ask, followed with "surely there are good Christians meeting in the other churches in the town?"

"Don't look on us as an example of what Christians should be," they would counter. "In fact," they would continue, "we're certain you'll find far better Christians in any church in Buckie than we will ever be."

"Why have you joined the Brethren sect then?" I would query.

"We don't believe we are a sect. You see Charles, to be sectarian you must rally round a particular denominational banner which denies the unity of the body of Christ. We are given the label 'The Brethren', or the 'Plymouth Brethren', but we do not own these sectarian definitions. We simply meet as brethren and sisters according to the clear teaching of the New Testament and born-again, baptised believers are welcome to meet with us, if they are prepared to bow to God's teaching."

One night I was convinced that I had a watertight argument against the views held by Davy.

"Listen Davy," I started with an air of self-confidence, "every denomination and religious group thinks they are right. Surely it is presumptuous to claim to be right and everybody else wrong?"

"You've never heard me making any boast

about being right?" The statement took the form of a question and I was conscious by the look in his eyes that he expected a reply, so I shook my head, for he was perfectly right. Peggy rose to put on the kettle sensing that the foundation had been laid for a lengthy discussion.

"I wasn't brought up within brethren circles, Charles," she said, pausing at the kitchen door. But I am where I am because the Word of God has directed me there."

"You see, Charles," Davy took up the theme, "God is surely more concerned than we are about the prevailing confusion. It is not His will that believers are not walking together in unity. Neither is it His desire that we remain in ignorance of His purposes and requirements. That's why he has given to us in His precious Word an unalterable pattern for meeting together in a church capacity. We need to get back to the simplicity of this pattern. In fact we need to get back to the simplicity of apostolic times. That's what actually happened during the last century."

"What happened then?" Davy's quiet sincerity always had a disarming effect on me, and I was anxious to learn.

"Well," he continued, "during the last century there was a widespread movement by which large numbers of God's people, some of them clergymen, physicians, titled men of high rank and barristers, broke free from the shackles of human tradition and met together as we do today. Mind you it must have taken great courage for them to have done this, for each denomination had been overgrown by a great variety of ritual promoted by generations of unchallenged usage. Together, those men of moral weight and intellectual power searched the Scripture. Helped by the Holy Spirit, they rediscovered beneath the ecclesiastical debris, a bedrock of truth, capable of guiding them in such matters as church gathering and practice. The amazing thing is that this happened in various localities simultaneously, each group being unaware of the other's existence. It was possible for Christians to conform to the truth then, and there's no doubt it is possible for them to do so today."

As Peggy handed round the sandwiches, I listened as Davy described how the brethren meetings were conducted without a presiding minister, thus recognising the priesthood of every believer. God-appointed, gifted men taught the Scriptures, and men of spiritual maturity cared for the welfare of the individual members of the church, (or assembly as it was usually called).

"But Davy you must agree that we are 'all one in Christ Jesus' and we should all be working together for the furtherance of the Gospel?" I queried.

"If you believe, and you obviously do, that sectarianism is wrong, how can our recognition of it be right? If it is not of God, then God cannot be pleased with our support of it, no matter how well-meaning our motives are. Remember what God said to Saul through Samuel in the Old Testament when Saul disobeyed God, although he meant well?"

I couldn't remember. "Obedience is better than sacrifice and to hearken than the fat of rams," he quoted when I didn't respond.

"You're a builder. You should know that if you deviate from the architect's plans you are in serious trouble." I noticed the twinkle in his eye as he continued. "Charles, just as Moses was given the plan of the Tabernacle in the Old Testament by God, so we today have a plan. In fact it is the only plan, and we deviate from it at our peril." Holding his Bible in front of him he went on to say with great emphasis, "In this Book we can find that plan. God wasn't taken unawares by the confusion we see around us today. His plan for church gathering is still as valid as it was in the days of the Apostles. God's great desire is that we search for that plan and seek to abide by it." Handing over the plate of sandwiches he said with a friendly grin, "How closely have you followed that plan so far?"

For several days my mind was a maelstrom of conflicting emotions. Sometimes I would dismiss what Davy had said as Pharisaical hypocrisy and sheer spiritual arrogance, and then I would search the New Testament to see what I could discover about the practice of the early Church. It became increasingly clear to me that a lot of what I had observed in the denominations had no backing whatsoever from the Word of God. I became convinced in my heart of hearts that the often despised people known as "brethren" were as near to the plan of church gathering as it could possibly be. Their church practice coincided as far as I could see, with the practice of the early Christians. But all my friends were in the Baptist Church. I had (and still have) the highest esteem for Mr. Barr. Grace by this time had been baptised and had linked herself with the believers who met in the Gospel Hall. I hated to think that if I followed her example, some would be tempted to think that I had severed my links with the denominations just to please her. I was in a real quandary.

The concept of a God-planned life looms largely in the teaching of Scriptures. I knew it was God's desire that I should know His will. In fact I knew that God commanded me to know His will. "Wherefore be not unwise, but understanding what the will of the Lord is" (Eph.5:17). To me that was as much a command as "Be ye reconciled to God." I knew God's will for me regarding church fellowship. But I was also reminded from the Scriptures that once His will was known I had to obey it: "as the servants of Christ, doing the will of God from the heart" (Eph.6:6). Then the personal words of the Lord Jesus pierced my heart as I read through the Gospel by John, chapter fourteen: "If ye love Me keep My commandments ... He that hath My command-ments, and keepeth them, he it is that loveth Me ... If a man love Me he will keep My words ... He that loveth me not keepeth not My sayings."

That settled the matter for me. I knew that I had reached a state of spiritual stagnation, because my knowledge of God's will had outstripped my obedience. I knew that my personal love for the Lord was now in the balance. In fact I was aware that unless I obeyed His Word, I had no right to call him "Lord". I weighed up the cost of disobedience in terms of lost communion, lack of spiritual progress, and effective witness to others. After much heart examination and prayer, I applied for fellowship in the Gospel Hall, Buckie.

The elders read to me, along with other portions of Scripture, the "blueprint of the Church", as they called it, from the Book of the Acts Chapter 2 Verses 41-42: "Then they that gladly received His word were baptised: and the same day there were added unto them three thousand souls. And they continued steadfastly in the apostles' doctrine and fellowship, and in breaking of bread, and in prayers." I was then asked several questions.

"Yes, I had received God's Word and had believed. No, I hadn't been baptised as a believer. Yes, I was prepared to accept the responsibilities as well as the privileges of being in fellowship."The date for my baptism was set and Grannie promised to be there.

# Chapter 14

## SPIRITUAL WARFARE

There was a great joy in my heart as I walked towards the Gospel Hall that cold wintry night. No joy, of course, can compare with the joy of knowing that one is pleasing the Lord. I had rid myself of my boxing trophies, and I had given my saxophone to my brother, for I was finished with my past life forever. Nobody had told me to do any such thing, and many Christians would probably have considered it a bit extreme, but then I alone knew the pull these things had upon my heart. I had far more important things to be occupied with, and I meant business with God. I was about to take a very important step in obedience to His will. I was about to be baptised by total immersion.

The hall was packed, and old Grannie, true to her word, was there. Quite a number of my relatives were sitting beside her. When I emerged out of the water everyone started to sing:

"When we walk with the Lord,
In the light of His Word,
What a glory He sheds on our way,
While we do His good will,
He abides with us still,
And with all who will trust and obey.

Trust and obey, for there's no other way
To be happy in Jesus, but to trust and obey."

The joy that was mine that night defies
definition. It was for Grace an extremely
emotional occasion, and, for kind souls like Davy
and Peggy, a time of great rejoicing. The
fellowship with the believers who gathered in the
plain, simply furnished hall, widened by spiritual
horizons almost immediately. I was at last
beginning to make spiritual progress.

But the spectre of unemployment was soon to
raise its head and blight our happiness. It was the
winter of 1957 and a "credit squeeze" had
virtually strangled the economy. With many
others I found myself in the "dole" queue.

After about twelve weeks I decided to go down
to Fleetwood to see if things were any better
there. Although I knew that Grannie would be
well enough looked after by her daughters round
about her, it was with great reluctance that I
waved goodbye to her. Grace knew that my being
out of work for so long had got me down and that I
wanted to regain my self-respect. But to be
suddenly cut off from her and the fellowship of
the believers, was a traumatic experience for me.

During the train journey I was overwhelmed
by feelings of loneliness. I spent most of the time
writing a lengthy letter to Grace. It was the first
letter of an intimate nature that I had ever
written, and I didn't find it very easy to express
my thoughts. But the separation was to give me
the opportunity to tell Grace my deepest feelings,

something that I just couldn't have done in her presence. As more and more letters were sent north in the following weeks, Grace was made aware that her patience and understanding had not been in vain.

I arrived at the terraced brick house late in the afternoon. After I had caught up with all the news my mother spoke up.

"We heard you were religious now."

Although one of the reasons for coming down to Fleetwood in search of work, was that I might witness to my parents about the Lord, this abrupt comment caught me unawares.

"Well," I smiled, slightly embarrassed, "I have accepted Christ as my own and personal Saviour, if that's what you mean." I knew that what I had said sounded a bit corny as I spoke to someone puffing smoke into my face.

"We're religious too you know." The words sounded rather incongruous, coming as they did between her drags on her cigarette. My surprised expression drew out some more surprising information.

"Sylvia started us off — she's Jimmie's girl-friend. Her mother is a well-known medium around here. We've had some great seances you know. We've had some messages from your grandad we have."

I stared in blank amazement. "You've what?"

"Oh yea, it's right enough, love. Would you like to join in our seance tonight? There may even be a message from your grandad 'cos he liked you, he did."

"But that sort of thing is Satanic, it's ..."

"Not at all. It's in the Bible," she broke in, flicking her cigarette-ash into the saucer nearby. She then gave, what I learned later to be a rather distorted account of King Saul's visit to the Witch of Endor. My knowledge of the Bible was too scant to make any protest. I knew very little about spiritualism at that time, but I knew enough to convince me that the whole thing was inspired by Satan. But how to convince my family was completely beyond me. Without a concordance I couldn't even turn to a verse referring to the subject. Oh! how I lamented my ignorance of the Word of God!

"Will you take part in our seance tonight, Charles, and you will be able to see for yourself that there's nothing to be frightened of?"

I feebly assented, not wishing to offend my mother, for I was indebted to her for agreeing to give me lodgings until I got some permanent work. I realise now that Satan was leading me into a subtle trap from which it would be very difficult to free myself by own resources. I had once heard how a spiritualist meeting couldn't proceed because a Christian was in the audience, and I smugly felt that my presence would ruin the seance.

Later that evening a small group was sitting around the big table in my mother's dining-room. The only light was a dim flow from the electric fire in the fireplace.

"Now, Charles," my mother began, "I will be acting as the medium. I will call upon the spirits to see if there is a message for anyone in this room. If there is, the table will lift three times and knock on the floor." A shiver went through me as I remembered three knocks many years earlier. The whole thing seemed unreal.

"Don't be frightened, love, when we make contact. Right then, let's put our hands on the table with our little fingers touching."

We placed our hands, palm down, on the table. My mother's voice spoke in a tremulous, respectful manner which was so different from her usual way of speaking.

"Is there a message for anyone in this room?"

I was glad that the room was reasonabaly dark, because my smile of amusement would not have been appreciated. I had to struggle to control myself as the plaintive, almost schoolgirlish voice asked with the ridiculous solemnity, "Is there a message for anyone in this room?" Instantly my smile was exchanged for a look of consternation. Three gentle knocks, as the table lifted, brought me back rudely to a state of stone-cold sobriety.

"There is a message, Charles," my mother whispered, "did you feel the table lifting?"

"No," I replied, as I tried to convince myself that the movements had been merely the nerves of my fingers playing tricks on me.

"Is there a message for anyone in this room?"

Again the girlish voice, but this time a little louder.

I wasn't prepared for what happened next. The table lifted in an unmistakable fashion, and literally thumped on to the floor three times.

Shaken with fright I stood up and switched on the light. The others were still sitting with their hands spread on the table.

"What you're doing isn't right. I'll have nothing to do with it," I said with a quivering lip.

My mother was livid with rage. "What on earth did you sit with us for, if you intended to break it off? You had no business taking part at all if you had no intentions of carrying on." She spat the words at me whilst I sat in the armchair, an abject figure without an answer to give.

I was very subdued for the rest of the evening. Sylvia tried to reassure me that there was nothing to fear. She told me that the spirits were kind and wanted to help us. They were our loved ones who had gone into the spirit world before us and were concerned about us. She went on to relate how she was cared for by guardian spirits when she was a child, and how they physically tucked her in bed at night. In fact she wouldn't sleep at night until these unseen "friends" had done this.

"How could evil spirits be so gentle and loving towards children, Charles? she asked.

Sylvia's mother had been active in the spiritualist movement for some time, and she herself had been nurtured on their teaching.

"Our church is just down at the bottom of the road. We have some wonderful times there. You'll be made very welcome," she went on.

"What form does your service take?" I was amazed to hear that there were such buildings. I had always associated spiritualism with dark rooms in private houses.

My mother, her anger abated, spoke up. "The meetings vary, but the ones I have attended are pretty straightforward. Everyone places an article, a thimble or even a button, belonging to themselves or a dead relative, on to a tray. When everybody has come in, the medium, usually a woman, takes up an article at random, and then passes on a message from the spirit world to the person who placed the article on the tray. Sometimes the medium's features are changed to the features of the person who has died and a direct conversation then takes place between the spirit of the dead person and the relative in the hall. They even speak the same way as they did when they were alive on earth."

I swallowed hard but said nothing. Before going to bed my mother made one final comment. "Remember, Charles, it could have been a message for you."

I went to bed, but not to sleep. I shared a bed with my brother Jimmie because of the shortage of room. I lay wide-awake all night. The presence of evil permeated the room. I thought of the reasons they had given for Jimmie's refusal to take part in the seance. He had been described as an excellent candidate for mediumship but his nerves had become affected. He decided to have no further part in any seances for he felt that he would end up in a mental hospital. And yet his future wife had defended spiritualism, and obviously believed that it was a God-given blessing to the world. As I pondered over the bizarre events of the previous evening, I felt that I was up against something too big for me to handle. As the hours of the night ticked past, and the sweat poured from my body, I made up my mind to take the first available train back to Buckie the following morning.

When morning finally arrived, I began to feel rather ashamed of myself. I pondered over the many times I had prayed for my family. I had now a wonderful opportunity to tell them personally of what the Lord had done for me. Now a brush with the evil powers of darkness had turned me into a coward, ready to run away. I thought of great men such as Dr.David Livingstone, who had entered the very strongholds of Satan in Africa, and had fearlessly proclaimed the Gospel story. Alone in that bedroom, tired out after a sleepless night, I bowed my knees in prayer: "Lord I feel too weak to cope with this problem, but please show me from Thy Word what I should do. Help me to show my family that they are being deceived by Satan, for I ask this in the Name of the Lord Jesus. Amen."

I sat on the edge of the bed and held my Bible. I was still virtually a babe in Christ, and I didn't know which part to turn to in order to find help in this moment of crisis. In my simplicity I had asked the Lord to show me from His Word the answer to my problem. I just opened my Bible and my eyes immediately caught the words, "Beloved, believe not every spirit, but try the spirits whether they are of God, because many false prophets are gone out into the world. Hereby

know ye the Spirit of God: Every spirit that
confesseth that Jesus Christ is come in the flesh is
of God; and every spirit that confesseth not that
Jesus Christ is come in the flesh is not of God; and
this is that spirit of antichrist, whereof ye have
heard that it should come, and even now already
is it in the world."

Although not very demonstrative, I could have
shouted HALLELUJAH a thousand times over. I
thanked the Lord from the depths of my heart for
hearing and answering my prayer. I dismissed
all cowardly notions of going home. I now felt that
the Lord had some business for me to do for Him.
With such a token of Divine intervention I now
felt able to face any difficulty.

When my mother asked me later on that day, if
I would like to take part in a seance that evening, I
readily consented.

"No backing out then," she warned.

"No backing out," I promised, then added, "I
want you to ask the spirit that you contact this
question immediately." I then read out to her the
question from the portion of Scripture that had
thrilled my soul that morning.

Her "O.K. by me," indicated that everything
was settled.

That evening the same group gathered around
the same table in the same dimly-lit room.

"Is there a message for anyone in this room?"
Again and again the question was asked without
the slightest tremor from the table.

"Funny, there was a message for someone
yesterday," she whispered. For fully ten minutes

she repeated her question, only to be met by a
deathly silence. I was convinced that Satan had
anticipated the question that my mother had
planned to ask, and his impersonating demons
had decided to avoid that particular seance. They
were not prepared to give assent to the incarnation
of Jesus, which of course is a foundational truth of
the Gospel.

Now I must strongly stress that I don't advise
any young Christian to open their Bibles at
random and attempt to find answers to their
problems in this way. I believe that God heard the
cry of a distressed babe in Christ, and came to my
aid that morning. I know of no portion of His Holy
Word that could have been more appropriate. It
revealed to me the fact that there is an unseen
spirit-world where there are both good and evil
spirits, and that the proof of their origin lay in
their testimony regarding the Person of Jesus. I
learned later that the interpretation of the passage
was far wider than I had realised. Just as it is
possible for a man to serve God in the power of the
Holy Spirit, so I learned, it was possible for false
teachers to serve Satan by turning people away
from the truth. In the days when the Church was
in its infancy, such false teachers crept in unawares, and this was the test to prove whether a
teacher's ministry was God-inspired. Unless he
confessed that Jesus was come in the flesh, he
manifested the spirit of antichrist.

I was given this passage by God, however, and I
felt perfectly justified in using it for the occasion.
I still feel that it can be used today to expose

spiritism, which is the proper description of this evil cult. I have met many who have dismissed my warnings about the dangers involved in dabbling with the occult. If they persistently refuse to listen, I challenge them to ask their contact in the spirit-world questions such as, "Did Jesus shed His blood on the cross to save sinners from Hell? Is it true that Satan is going to be cast into the Lake of Fire? Is Jesus, King of Kings and Lord of Lords, God over all blessed forever?" Whilst I would never encourage anyone to take part in any occult activity, for those who are already involved, these questions would soon discover the real source of the spirits they are in contact with.

Although I was a little upset about the table being raised in my presence, I learned soon afterwards that many a young Christian has been lured away from the faith by seducing spirits. Who knows what could have happened if my "grandfather" had spoken to me? As many people have genuinely been healed at such meetings, Who knows what I would have done if I had been healed of my dreaded psoriasis? It would have been very difficult to believe that such a miracle had been performed through a demonic agency. I had gone into a seance-room in a prayerless state of smug, self-complacency. I believe the Lord was there to deliver a weak, ignorant child in the faith, and was prepared to help that child win a victory over the powers of darkness that he could never have won for himself. None of us have even begun to understand the great power of Satan our subtle adversary. We can only resist him with the help of the One Who is All-Powerful and Who has given to us for our protection the whole armour of God. Let none presume to think that all the Christian needs to make a spiritist meeting ineffective, is to have a Bible in their pocket or to speak flippantly about the blood of Christ. Let such remember well the great powers of the Egyptian magicians in Moses' day. Let them never forget the massacre of God's own people, who dared to treat the Ark of God as a kind of lucky charm to assure them of victory over the Philistines. Even Michael the Archangel acknowledged that Satan's power was not something to be treated lightly.

Not long after this, I acquired a booklet written by A.J. Pollock on the subject. The Lord used this to open the eyes of my family to the diabolical nature of spiritism. They were able to see from God's Word that such practices were condemned time and time again. From then on there were no more seances held in the home, and as far as I know, they didn't go back to the larger meetings in the church. (I was delighted to hear later that the building was sold to an evangelical group, who preach the Gospel of the Grace of God.)

My stay in Fleetwood didn't last very long. The work situation was just as bad there. I managed to get a job as a postman during the Christmas period and was offered a permanent post. But by this time I was missing Grace very much, and so I headed north before the year was out.

For a short time I worked as a milkroundsman

and then I was offered a job with my old building firm. With other young Christians who were ardent students of the Word of God, I was invited to various homes. There the Scriptures were discussed and many a discussion extended into the early hours of the morning. We all had an insatiable thirst for the Word. On Friday evenings, all the young men from various assemblies along the coast converged on the home of a Mr.Logie, who conducted consecutive Bible studies. One could not be in such an environment and not make spiritual progress. It wasn't long before every young brother was preaching the Gospel, and ministering the Word of God to the edification of the believers. Those were indeed balmy days, and my relationship with Grace blossomed amidst such warmth of Christian love and fellowship.

# Chapter 15

## TOGETHER-FOREVER

As Grannie was becoming more infirm, Grace
and I started to plan our wedding. The net-loft
was no longer required as Grannie's mending
days were over. We decided to make it into a nice
little flat. One day I found Grannie very upset and
I soon got her tearful story, to the effect that I had
no claim on the property, and I would be wasting
my money by modernising the loft. The property
had been willed to other members of the family by
my grandfather, and Grannie had only her
lifetime of the house. She tearfully advised me to
look elsewhere for somewhere to set up my own
home. But to leave the only mother that I had ever
known was totally unthinkable. Grace and I
prayed about the matter. We decided to contact
the relatives concerned and they offered to have
the house valued as it was. If I would pay off the
bond and give them the balance when Grannie
died, the house would be mine. Needless to say we
were overjoyed.

One of the most touching moments of my life
was when I handed the recovered title-deeds of
the house into Grannie's hand. I had worked hard
and very slowly raised the amount. Tears
streamed down her cheeks, dripping over the
care-worn wrinkles, as she clutched the precious

"My Grace..." Wedding Day Smiles

documents that she hadn't seen since she was a young woman.

Grace and I both hated debt, so we took some time to modernise the house. We just did a little at a time as we could afford it. In fact there was quite a lot still to be done when we got married, but it was our own home, we were comfortable, and above all we were very happy.

We spent our honeymoon in Bangor, Northern Ireland. We stayed in a delightful Christian guest house near the sea front. We enjoyed the fellowship of the Christians very much, and the highlight of our honeymoon was the beautiful day when a Mr.Cowie, himself a Buckie man resident in Bangor, took us all round the Antrim coast in a car. It is still a great source of amusement to us when we remember that the first night of our honeymoon was spent in the palatial Gloucester Hotel in Aberdeen and our last night, in a cold draughty waiting-room in Aberdeen Station — flat broke but happy.

Our first boy we called Stephen. Grannie seemed to get a new lease of life when he came along, and she simply spoiled him. She insisted that she would babysit to let us out to the meetings together.

As a family we have shared some harrowing experiences together. On one occasion, Stephen had to be rushed by ambulance to the Sick Children's Hospital in Aberdeen with a very high temperature. The specialist who attended to him had noticed some extensive bruises on his body and had suspected leukaemia. We had secretly feared the worst ourselves, having been told that such bruising was a symptom of the illness. We received word to come in to the hospital for the specialist wanted to talk to us about Stephen. We were now sure that our worst fears were realised, and we went to Aberdeen with heavy hearts. We could only cast ourselves upon the Lord and commit Stephen into His care, for we were at our wit's end. How we thanked the Lord when the specialist told us that, although leukaemia had been suspected, all the tests proved negative.

Our reading of the Scriptures and the giving of thanks for our food had become an accepted custom in our house. Grannie was usually quite happy to have her meals with us even when we had visiting preachers. The old hatred for our neighbours across the street gradually disappeared, and in fact a warm friendship developed. One day I visited Grannie, who had been taken to her daughter's home because Grace was well advanced with our second child. During the conversation she looked up into my face.

"Charles, I want to tell you something," she whispered. I knew that we wouldn't have Grannie for long, and I thought that she wanted to tell me something about the disposal of her few earthly possessions. Or it could be something about her funeral arrangements. Anyway I put my head almost on her pillow as I waited for her to proceed.

"Charles," she continued, "I want to let you know that I have received the Lord Jesus as my Saviour too." I couldn't speak. Tears of joy soaked the pillow as old Grannie and I shared a few moments too private to describe. On my way out I told my aunt what Grannie had just told me and she confirmed her story. The previous night a Christian lady had visited the home and had taken the opportunity to speak to Grannie about her eternal welfare. Old Grannie had made her peace with God there and then, and here she was testifying to me. A couple of weeks later, on the verge of her eighty-sixth year, Grannie was called home to be with the Lord forever. Who has dared to say that the age of miracles is past?

In 1964 I decided to start in business on my own account. I bought an old pick-up truck for fifty pounds and advertised in our local paper that I was available for work. To get established I tackled everything that was offered, ranging from house repairs to window-cleaning and sweeping chimneys. Before long I had a nice little business employing two other workmen.

I was in the house one day when Grace came into the room.

"Some men want to see you," she announced.

Outside stood two builders from my old firm, one being the foreman who had treated me so badly.

"We were wondering if you could help us. Things are getting tight in the firm and there's no overtime." The foreman shuffled his feet around a stone uneasily. "Think you could give us some work to do?"

My mind flashed back to that cruel winter. The lonely hours spent as an outcast inside a metal cover. The insults and the time I had spent in "Coventry". For a brief moment a wave of resentment entered my heart to be as quickly dispelled by a greater power; the power of love. I realised that it hadn't been easy for these men to have come to me with such a request. I needed no apology, for their action had said it all as far as I was concerned.

"Sure. As a matter of fact I'm under a bit of pressure just now to get work completed. I would appreciate your help very much."

# Chapter 16

## SAVED TO SERVE

If I were to be asked what I considered to be the two most distinctive features of the so called "open" brethren I would say it is firstly a love for God's Word and secondly an interest in spreading the Gospel at home and abroad. They probably boast more missionaries per membership head than any other group that comes under the umbrella term of Christianity. A prayer list is printed annually containing a great number of names of missionaries —many of whom are doctors, nurses and teachers. Without any fixed salary, and looking to the Lord to supply their needs through His people, they have left the comforts and relative security of the homelands to serve God in foreign lands. A booklet entitled *Echoes of Service* is published every month, giving vital information about the various work being carried on in the mission field. It tells of the missionary's successes, failures, disappointments and aspirations, and stimulates prayer and practical interest within the hearts of the believers at home.

I'm sure that most keen Christians have had a desire to become a missionary at one time or another. This is sometimes just a passing phase or merely the short term result of hearing a stirring missionary report. I was no different. I realised, however, that my faith wasn't strong enough to go out without any visible support, especially having a dependent wife and three young children. I remember reading that there were opportunities for suitably qualified teachers in several Third World countries. But I had left the school at fifteen without any qualifications whatsoever. I had a family and a business to look after, with little or no time to study anything but my Bible. And yet I couldn't get the idea out of my mind. I would like to serve the Lord as a teacher near to a mission station. The idea became almost an obsession when I read of a special Recruitment Scheme for mature students, who wanted to become teachers.

"If any man lack wisdom, let him ask of God, that giveth to all men liberally, and upbraideth not; and it shall be given to him." I read these words in the Epistle of James Chapter 1 Verse 5. I read it again and again. No, I wasn't misreading and I believed it meant exactly what it said. God was prepared to give wisdom to those who asked in sincerity and with a worthy motive. I decided to enrol for evening classes.

Mr.McIntosh seemed a little harassed as he tried to explain to the group of potential candidates the various subjects available, and the evenings when they would be held. I felt a little self-conscious as I stood at the fringe of the group wondering whether or not I should be there. Then I remembered God's promise to those that ask

Him for wisdom. I remembered how I had stood for an hour in a dark corner of the school building praying to the Lord that He would shut the door of opportunity rather than let me take a wrong step, and not only make a fool of myself, but also bring discredit to the testimony. Fortified in this way, I had mustered up enough courage to join this eager group of aspiring academics.

"The English class will be held on Wednesday night in room seven," Mr.McIntosh said as he scanned the cluster of faces around him. Wednesday night was out as far as I was concerned for we held our Prayer Meeting then. I slowly edged towards the door of the class-room, hoping that no-one would notice my rather inglorious exit. The Lord had closed the door — or so I thought.

I had just come to the room seven referred to by Mr.McIntosh, and was about to turn round the corner and go out into the night when a loud shout stopped me in my tracks.

"Where are you running off to Mr.Geddes!?"
It was the voice of Mr.McIntosh and the empty corridor seemed to amplify it. He had obviously seen me in the group and watched my disappearing act. I had worked at his house on several occasions, so I was no stranger to him.

"Sorry, Mr. McIntosh, but our Prayer Meeting is held on a Wednesday night, so it's no use," I replied. I was about to make a joke about being over-ambitious when he interrupted.

"Come back here and we'll see if another night would be more suitable for the others."

12

Graduation.

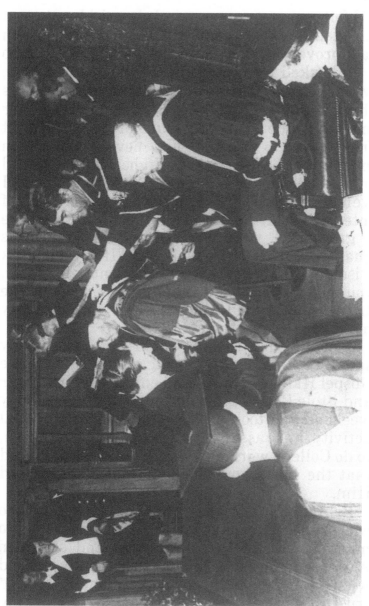

"Having therefore obtained help of God"
Capping ceremony. Marischal College. Aberdeen.

I felt every eye upon me as I sheepishly retraced my steps into the room. But another night did in fact prove to be more suitable for everyone and so I embarked on my evening-class studies. God, without the slightest doubt, helped me to pass three Highers. Sometimes I could only attend for one term due to the pressure of work, and yet from start to finish I had never to resit an examination. Another three Highers were obtained in the College of Commerce, Aberdeen, where I went for a year. This was followed by four years of intensive study in the College of Education where I graduated with a B.Ed. degree, and was qualified to teach three subjects. "If any man lack wisdom ...?" When many apparently brighter, younger students had fallen by the wayside the Lord brought me through. All praise and glory must be His, and His alone.

I made sure that I would not neglect my spiritual life. Every week I attended the little Gospel Hall at Footdee and enjoyed their Prayer and Bible Reading. I came home to Buckie every weekend and took my full share of the spiritual activity in the assembly. I resisted the temptation to do College work on a Sunday. I was convinced that the Lord would honour me if I honoured Him.

Behind me there was also a devoted wife who was prepared to make great sacrifices in order to make it possible for me to go and study in Aberdeen. It was much later that I really learned what it cost her in terms of loneliness and frustration with a growing family making constant demands upon her. But she hid all this from me so that I would not be distracted from my studies.

Thrown together with hundreds of students and lecturers of all persuasions, brought many opportunities to witness for the Lord. It certainly wasn't all plain sailing, especially when one was confronted by an extremely articulate opponent of the Gospel. But the Lord helped me time and time again.

I remember the occasion when one of the lecturers was maintaining that it was sheer presumption to claim to be saved in the evangelical sense. I immediately stated that I knew I was saved and bound for Heaven and that it was also possible for everyone in the classroom to have this assurance as well.

"Now, now, Mr.Geddes," he went on in a rather patronising manner, "we must always be asking existential questions and seeking for revelatory answers. Life is a continual search for meaning and understanding. It's like walking a tightrope tied at one end with faith and the other end with doubt and fear."

"But Jesus said, 'Verily, verily, I say unto you, he that heareth My words, and believeth on Him that sent Me, HATH everlasting life, and SHALL NOT come into condemnation; but IS passed from death unto life.' I prefer to believe what Jesus said, and this removes all doubts and fears from me," I replied.

Getting a little impatient, the lecturer snapped; "Yes, but what we should say is, 'Lord, I believe —

help mine unbelief,' and if we adopt that humble position I believe we are on safe ground."

"No," I immediately responded, "I don't say these words at all as far as salvation is concerned. I say what the man in John's Gospel said, 'One thing I know, that, whereas I was blind, now I see,' and I don't call it presumption either."

Such exchanges were fairly frequent, and the views of some of the students who were being trained to teach Religious Education in schools filled me with considerable alarm. On one occasion I was told by one lecturer that my contributions were holding up the progress of the class, and that I must remain silent. Claiming to be saved or converted apparently was viewed as a distinct handicap as far as the teaching of Religious Education was concerned. It was generally believed that a committed Christian could not adopt an open-ended approach to teaching. Everyone else, whether he be atheist, agnostic or even a Communist could be unbiased, but not the Christian. It really proved to me how naive some people in places of authority can be, and also their ignorance of the fact that only God can effect a work of grace in a person's heart, be he a pupil or otherwise.

For part of my spell in Aberdeen I had a room in the Y.M.C.A. Young people from all parts of the world stayed there. Some of them were very homesick and were glad to talk with me after dinner at night. I remember one African, wide eyed and chuckling with great delight as I sang in Swahili the words of the chorus: "All the way to

Calvary He went for me - He died to set me free."
Close friendships were formed, and when some of
them went back to their own countries it was an
emotional affair.

For two consecutive summers I went with
Mr.Harold German, the well-known evangelist,
to various places in Cumbria. This must have put
an extra strain on Grace after the long periods of
absence in Aberdeen, but she never complained,
but rather encouraged me. Our first Gospel
campaign together, was in a hall located in the
Hensingham housing estate in Whitehaven.
There, for about six weeks we preached the dear
old story of a Saviour's love to both adults and
children. We stayed in a little caravan that was
parked near the hall. It was a real spiritual uplift
to me to spend so much time with a faithful
warrior of the cross, who had been preaching
fulltime for over fifty years. He had been greatly
used of God during his many years of service, and
he was still bearing fruit in his old-age. A woman
was saved on the very first night of the meetings
under his preaching.

On one occasion I gave a lesson to the children,
based on the story of Naaman. I had closed the
meeting in prayer and had thanked them for
coming. As they started moving out past Mr.
German who was at the door, I started to gather
all the bits and pieces of the flannel-graph that I
had been using. Then from the corner of my eye I
noticed that the front row of girls remained
seated.

"What is it girls?" I asked, taken aback a little.

"Please, Mr. Geddes, we want to be cleansed from our sin. We want to get saved."

I immediately gestured to Mr. German to come down to the front of the hall, but his keen eye had already taken in the situation, and he just shook his head and pointed back at me. Well, I had spoken to individuals before about their soul's salvation, but here were six young girls all quietly waiting for me to speak to them. I had always been very wary about young children in case I gave them some false hope, based on a mere emotional profession. I had avoided all forms of appeal at the end of the story of Naaman. I had asked the Lord to do His own work in the hearts of these young people. When I sat down beside them I soon discovered that the Lord had done just that. They were obviously very aware of their sinful state before God, and were desirous of His salvation. It was a simple matter, as it always is, to point the seeking sinner to the seeking Saviour. My joy knew no bounds that day for there is no joy quite like that of leading souls to Christ. It was indeed a time of great blessing for us all, and I shall never forget the kindness of the Christians of this area of Cumbria.

The following year I went with Mr. German to the little district of Aiketgate, and also to the city of Carlisle. This was a campaign of contrasts. Part of the time was spent working around the quiet, sleepy hamlet with its beautiful scenery, and the rest of the time was spent trudging round the nearest thing to the concrete jungle situation that I've ever come across. Poor Mr.

German was literally worn out as we went round thousands of doors with tracts, and invited the people to come to the meetings. Although the saints were encouraged, I was disappointed that there was so little fruit to show for so many weeks of hard work.

As I was away for eight weeks on this occasion one can imagine the extra strain on Grace. I had been tempted to spend my vacation building a bungalow or two, as there was a tremendous building boom in progress, but Grace and I felt that building for eternity was a far better investment. Our eyes were by this time on a particular area of Zambia, called Mwinilunga, where some of our own missionaries had been praying for a Christian teacher to come to the school there. We both felt that my experience with Mr.German would stand me in good stead there. But apart from that we fully appreciated that God was no man's debtor, and we have proved this to be true.

# Chapter 17

## BLESSING OR CURSE?

One day a very cheery, fair-haired young man appeared in the Y.M.C.A. I observed him for a few days and I noticed that he had a great interest in everyone. I decided to deliberately sit beside him at the dinner table to hear what he had to say.

"Do you know that the Lord loves you?" he asked a big man from Nigeria. The African just smiled and carried on with his meal as the stranger, with beaming face, told him the story of Jesus and His death on the cross for sinners. What struck me was that he spoke in such a fashion that it was almost impossible to be offended by him.

Later that evening I got him on his own and started firing questions at him. Where did he come from? What religious group was he attached to? What was he doing in the Y.M.C.A.? I learned that he came from Fraserburgh and that he was linked with the Pentecostal "Assembly of God" there. He had given up a prosperous job at the fishing and was doing painting work in order to serve the Lord more fully. He had offered to paint the Y.M.C.A. premises, and that was why he was staying there for a short time. I immediately challenged him on the matter of "speaking in tongues".

"Look," he said firmly, "we have about seventy

men in this place, and as far as I can see they are all on their way to Hell. We have a little mission-field all to ourselves here. What about forgetting about tongues, and everything else that we don't agree about, and try to win these men for the Lord? Let's really give ourselves to prayer and see if something can be done." The genuine concern of this young man and his transparent sincerity completely disarmed me. After a day spent in secular study with ungodly men, it was like a breath of fresh air to meet a man with such noble ambitions.

And we did pray together. When I was free at night we would meet in his room and sing all the choruses we knew. We would go over any spiritual thoughts that we had gleaned from the Word of God, and then we would really get down to specific prayer on behalf of our fellow residents. I must say in all truthfulness that it was a revelation to me to hear the heart-rending sobs of a man, whose heart was almost breaking because lost souls were heading for "the blackness of darkness forever". The bedcovers were literally soaked by the tears of this young man who had come from a very poor background himself, but had experienced the wondrous joy of sins forgiven.

On one occasion two Chinese men knocked on the bedroom door and asked if they could join us. They had heard a chorus that they had heard many years earlier in the Salvation Army in their own country. We had a great opportunity to witness to them about the Lord. One night a

young man couldn't sleep because of the heavy
burden of sin upon his heart. Although it was very
late he came and knocked on my friend's door and
told him he wanted to get saved, and, praise God,
he got saved! And so in this way we endeavoured
to sow the seed of the Word of God, and left the
results with Him. My friend often went out at
night to speak to young people as they came out of
discos and other places of amusement, but I was,
of course, tied with my studies. I had been
neglecting them for a few weeks and they all
seemed to be getting on top of me.

Perhaps this had something to do with the
rather barren period that I began to pass through
at this time. Perhaps the continual bombardment
of non-spiritual material upon my mind had at
last caught up with me. Whatever the reason, my
dissatisfaction with my own state of soul was
thrown into greater relief, by the unquenchable
fervour and passion for souls of my new-found
brother in Christ. I had never met anyone with his
zeal before, and his warm, loving concern for
other people, drew out my highest admiration.
His natural flow of speech as he talked about a
person's deep need as a sinner before God, the way
he would put an arm around their shoulder, the
winning smile; all this marked him out as an
outstanding personal evangelist. He was completely obsessed with one objective, and that was
to win souls. He was also the most unworldly
prayerful believer that I had ever come across.
He had only one topic of conversation — Christ
and His salvation.

And yet this brother claimed that this hadn't always been the case. There was a time in his early Christian life when he found it extremely difficult to hand out a Gospel tract, or speak to anyone about eternal matters. He claimed that an experience called the "Baptism in the Holy Spirit" revolutionised his whole life. I had heard of this before and in fact I had just read a book *The Cross and the Switchblade* by David Wilkerson, where this same experience was referred to. In my studies at the College I had looked at a wide range of different religious expressions, and this had been included.

There is within the framework of every religious group a great variety of opinions, some minor, some fundamental. The Pentecostal groups are no different. Some believe that every person is saved and bound for Heaven the moment they accept the Lord Jesus as their Saviour, but then again, others don't. Some believe that a person receives the Holy Spirit at the moment of conversion, whilst others disagree. But nearly all of them believe that the "baptism in (or of) the Holy Spirit" is subsequent to conversion, and, although not essential to enable one to get to Heaven, is essential for effective Christian witness.

Now, there would be something far wrong if a Christian didn't want to be used of God in effective witness, and I certainly wanted the very best that God had to offer. For a time, as I passed through this barren period, I genuinely wondered whether or not I had somehow missed something

in my Christian life. I certainly bemoaned my
lack of power in witnessing for the Lord. In
several areas of my life, I realised that I wasn't
really what I should be. I had been aware that
Christians were commanded to "be filled with the
Spirit" (Eph.5:18). In the Book of Acts, I had
observed that Christians such as Stephen and
Barnabas were distinguished from other Christians, because they were "full of the Holy Ghost". I
had also read the biographies of great men of God
such as D.L.Moody and the saintly George
Müller. Both of them describe a crisis moment in
their Christian experiences, the outcome of
which, altered their whole course of service for
God. "Could this 'baptism' referred to be merely
the Pentecostal label for the same thing?" I asked
myself. There was certainly no evidence that they
spoke in tongues, so that was of no consequence as
far as I was concerned. But power to witness I
desperately wanted, and I felt that the obvious
lack of it was directly linked with the failure to
give the Holy Spirit His proper place in my life. It
was just as if a builder had sold a house and had
refused to give the purchaser every key of his
property. I knew that the Lord had bought me
with His precious blood, but somehow I felt that I
hadn't surrendered every department of my life to
Him.

I knew that the Charismatic Movement was
sweeping across the world. I was convinced that
the so-called healing gifts had no support from
the Word of God. The Apostle Paul had some very
close friends and fellow labourers in the Gospel.

Although he once had the gift of healing, he couldn't use it to heal his dearest friend and son in the faith, Timothy. Instead he advised him not to drink water but "use a little wine for thy stomach's sake and thine often infirmities." (1 Tim.5:23). Then again, he had to leave a faithful fellow worker sick at Miletum. (2 Tim.4:20). But my friend at the Y.M.C.A. definitely had a power to witness that I certainly didn't possess, and the more I desired it the more miserable I became. I reached the lowest ebb of my Christian experience, and, in a state of mental and spiritual distress I again cast myself on the Lord, and gave myself wholeheartedly to the searching of the Word of God. I re-examined the words of the Lord through the Apostle in 1 Corinthians. I had no reason to doubt what I earlier had accepted, that when Paul was writing, only a small part of the New Testament was then in existence. In order to supply the great need of the early Church, the Lord had given certain gifts such as Prophecy and Knowledge until that which was "perfect" had come. These gifts were "in part" and were to be done away, and when the New Testament was finally completed, that which was perfect had come. In all integrity I could not accept any other interpretation. The perfect, revealed mind of God "had come", and there is no need for the temporary gifts, for they have served their purpose.

I also noted God's desire regarding the role of women in the church at Corinth. It was as plain as God could make it that the women had to keep silent in the church, for it was not permitted for them to speak. I had heard the argument that the word "speak"in 1 Corinthians Chapter 14 Verse 34 was the same as the word "chatter" and was simply a local problem that Paul was dealing with. I was aware, of course, that the same word was used in other parts of the chapter and made this argument rather foolish, for we should expect the prophets to be "chattering" at the express command of the Apostle Paul, "Let the prophets speak."(verse 29). The Holy Spirit could not possibly have inspired the Apostle to write: "It is a shame for a woman to speak in the church," and then exercise such to speak, whether in tongues or otherwise in a church gathering. The Holy Spirit always rides in the chariot of the Word of God and He can never contradict Himself. So, in spite of my great admiration for my zealous brother in the Lord, and my own personal desire for the fulness of God's blessing upon my life, the unchangeable, impregnable rock of the Word of God proved once again to be the only safe place for my pilgrim feet. Make no mistake, I have still a great regard for my brother, and for all the dear saints who are linked with the Charismatic Movement, but I'm more convinced than ever now, that their path is a slippery one that can lead them on to all sorts of God-dishonouring excesses.

One grave danger where there is any form of self-abandonment, is the real possibility of falling prey to the evil spirits referred to in 1 Timothy Chapter 4 Verse 1, "Now the Spirit speaketh expressly that in the latter times some shall depart from the faith, giving heed to seducing spirits". Since the "speaking in tongues" cult finds its supporters amongst spiritists, Mormons, Roman Catholics and a number of heathen religious groups, every child of God should be very careful.

Perhaps the most subtle danger associated with this "baptism" or "second blessing", as some call it, lies in the danger of those who fail to receive it becoming extremely distressed. I was to learn that many fine Christians were driven to irreparable despair because they were continually frustrated in their desire to receive it at "tarrying meetings". They began to look upon themselves as second-class Christians. The more they yearned for it and failed to receive it, the more dejected they became, and a vicious circle was formed. They always blamed their own lack of faith or faithfulness to God, and the end product was a miserable useless creature who had lost his or her joy in the Lord.

Although I know that my friend was an exception to the rule and certainly did not give top priority to the so-called gifts, I discovered that the be-all-and-end-all of mainstream Pentecostalism is the exercising of these. Generally speaking the speaking in tongues is to them the evidence that one has received the "baptism". One particular girl I met at the College was completely obsessed with the desire to speak in tongues. She became more and more unhappy as the weeks went past. The impartial observer would be forced to admit

13

that such an unhappy state of mind was not the Lord's will for His children. The sad thing is that it is always the sincere, earnest Christian, who wants to move on with the Lord, who becomes the victim of such a situation. Would that we all realised more fully that we have been blessed with "*all* spiritual blessings in Heavenly places in Christ" (Eph.1:3).

Once we come to realise that we have a subtle enemy, ever seeking to destroy our witness for Christ and to rob us of our joy, we can be on our guard. But it is usually when we are on the mountain-top that he attacks. It was just after I had come to terms with this "baptism" question and was again enjoying sweet communion with the Lord that I was heckled by a "tongues" woman, who happened to be in the audience in a Gospel Hall when I was preaching the Gospel. She was along with a few others of the same persuasion, and she interrupted me in a rather embarrassing fashion. Had there been any unconverted people in to hear the Gospel they most assuredly would have been stumbled by such unbecoming behaviour. Her actions only served to reinforce in my mind what I had arrived at earlier from the Word of God.

# Chapter 18

## HIS WAY IS PERFECT

Graduation day came on the fourth of July 1974. My family could say, "The Lord hath done great things for us whereof we are glad." Apart from the Lord's help and the many sacrifices that my wife and family had to make, the whole enterprise would have been absolutely impossible.

The occasion was, however, tinged with disappointment. The Zambian authorities in London had given me every encouragement every time I communicated with them about my intentions. I had applied for a teaching post in Mwinilunga, and I knew of course that there was a vacancy there. I had made it clear to them that I was prepared to get involved in any extra-curricular activities, where my skills as a builder would be used to the full. They seemed quite pleased about that, but their last letter to me asked if I knew anyone in this area, and my reasons for wanting a post there. I didn't want to hide anything, and I knew that if the Lord wanted me there I wouldn't need to creep in by a back door. I told them that I was a committed Christian who wanted to help them in any way I could. I mentioned my prayerful interest in the Mission Station in the area. Although I didn't know any of the missionaries personally, I mentioned their names from the prayer-list. For weeks there was no response and I wrote again to no avail. On several occasions I made lengthy telephone calls to their offices in London. Each time I was passed from one person to another, without making any headway at all. In desperation I finally wrote and gave them an ultimatum. I gave them a date by which to give me a reply one way or other. I reminded them that I had a family to consider, and I would have to secure a post in this country very soon if they didn't co-operate. No reply was ever received.

I have always marvelled at those Christians who seem to find the will of God an easy thing to determine, as far as their own personal lives are concerned. I know that God's will can be established from His Word, from the inner promptings of the Holy Spirit, and also from external circumstances. The easy-going Christian, who is quite content to drift through life, has no problems at all of course. They've never asked the question, "Lord, what wilt Thou have me to do?" They've never looked on the fields and seen them white already to harvest. They've never been prostrated in agonising prayer because the labourers are so few. They've never spent sleepless nights because men die in darkness at their side without a hope to cheer the tomb. It never occurs to them to gaze upon a perishing world and say to the Lord, "Here am I, send me." Many such, live their lives as if money and material comforts were the main aims in life. They live and act as if the royal route to happiness was written only on the back of a pound note.

On the other hand it is possible to manufacture circumstances and then afterwards tag on the label, "The Lord's Will", to justify our actions. After re-assessing my motives for going in for further education before the Lord, I was given the inward peace and assurance that God's glory had been uppermost, and I could look forward with confidence knowing that the Lord would be with me in whatever sphere of service He Himself would choose.

One is learning daily that God has never assured us of an easy passage — only a safe landing. The great Apostle Paul's life was marked by struggle and conflict. The presence of God with him did not mean that he was lifted up above the storms, the tempests and the afflictions of life. His was a long and bitter struggle against the powers of Hell, malicious and jealous brethren, and many physical calamities. From it all he emerged victorious in the power of the One Who strengthened him. But even the Apostle himself must have had difficulty in discerning the Lord's will for him.

In his preaching journeys he wanted to go to Asia to preach the Word, but he and his companions were forbidden. Then they wanted to bring the Good News to Bithynia, but the Spirit suffered them not. (Acts 16:6-7). When he was scourged and cast into the inner prison at Philippi, he could well have been excused if he had felt that he had somehow mistaken God's will, in spite of the vision he had received. Now there can be no doubts about the purity of Paul's motives. He had suffered the loss of all things in order to follow the path of the once crucified, now glorified Christ. He had no lack of spiritual perception for obviously he was a spiritual giant. The sum of the matter is simply this, that even the godliest of men may confuse their own wills with the will of God. If such as Paul could encounter difficulty then I felt justified in consoling myself. I had to learn that our stops as well as our steps are ordered by the Lord, and that the disappointments are His appointments. As a family we were prepared to yield, follow and obey, irrespective of what avenues of service His unfolding will would eventually reveal.

Since 1974 it has been my inestimable privilege to teach the Word of God to pupils in Lossiemouth, Forres and Buckie. The number of pupils who have been under my supervision now run into several thousands. Much prayer from many quarters, has gone up to the Throne of Grace on their behalf. The Seed was sown daily and I believe God can do His own work in their hearts, for "Faith cometh by hearing and hearing by the Word of God."

Among the visiting speakers that I have invited into the school have been missionaries from Thailand, India, Japan, Ethiopia, Italy, Africa and other evangelists from the British Isles and other European countries. All have taken the opportunity to tell what God is doing, and still can do, not only in far off lands, but also in the particular school where they were speaking.

I have been greatly encouraged by the many who have assured me that they were upholding me daily in prayer. They fully appreciated the tremendous opportunities presented to me in teaching the Scriptures to about a thousand pupils throughout the whole school year as was the case in my recent post at Buckie. Our timetable week lasted for a fortnight, made possible because the school year was divided up into blocks, each lasting for a fortnight. As the older pupils left and younger ones came from the Primary School it also meant an entirely new group every four or five years. Since I've started teaching, a few have professed faith in the Lord Jesus. I would dearly have loved to have seen more but I believe that is God's affair not mine. Who can tell what the Spirit of God can do in the coming years in the hearts of those who heard the Word of God for five consecutive years? His Word cannot return unto Him void. Yes, the Lord has more than compensated for my disappointment about Zambia.

It hasn't been easy of course. One had to be prepared to be a "fool for Christ" every day. One couldn't persistently condemn the rising interest in the occult without incurring some kind of opposition. One cannot continually exalt the Person of Christ and be free from hostile pressures. Indeed the enemy has sometimes come in like a flood and brought almost unbearable pressure to bear upon me. Oh, I have much to thank my prayer-partners for! Without their help I'm sure I would have given in many a time.

Some of the worst trouble that I've encountered has come from pupils who were brought up on a praying-mother's knee and have heard the Gospel since infancy. One of the worst pupils of this category was a Hopeman boy. He was in the rowdiest class in the Lossiemouth school and he was the ringleader. I had him during his last year at school and he was determined to make a nuisance of himself every time he came to me for Religious Education. He stirred up the rest of the class and took great pleasure in mocking the claims of God upon his life. One day he delighted his pals by boasting that he knew that the Bible was full of rubbish.

"That's interesting," I said, as I held out the Bible to him, "just show us all an example of the rubbish that you speak about."

He wasn't quite sure what to do but the other members of the class spoke up in chorus, "Go on, Jim, show him!"

Faced with the challenge he realised that he had to do something, so he sauntered out to the floor and opened the Bible indiscriminately and pointed to a spot on a page with a dramatic flourish of his hand. I held his hand against the page and prevented him from returning to his seat for I had recognised the verse to which he had pointed.

"Now read out to the class what you consider to be rubbish," I said firmly. The class again shouted their encouragement to their hero.

He started to read but the words withered on his lips and they tailed off to a quiet slur.

"Well, since you won't read out your example of rubbish from the Bible, I will," I said as I still held his finger on to the place.

"The verse that Jim has chosen to prove that the Bible is full of rubbish is found in John's Gospel Chapter 8 Verse 24 and reads: 'I said therefore unto you, that ye shall die in your sins: for if ye believe not that I am He, ye shall die in your sins'."

I read the verse over again and warned the young man that because of his privileges he was more responsible before God than the others. He was quiet for the rest of the period and stayed behind to ask a few questions about the reality of conversion. I don't know if he ever put his trust in the Lord but I know he was startled by that experience and was never as rowdy again.

It is interesting to note that my own classroom in Buckie High School, where I was the Principal Teacher of Religious Education, was number seven. It was outside this room that I was stopped when I tried to leave the enrolment-class session many years earlier. How often we have to acknowledge that "His ways are past finding out".

As can be appreciated, the account of my experiences with the many pupils in different schools during the last years would fill a volume itself. There have been pupils from broken homes, disaster-hit fishing families; pupils with real emotional and spiritual problems, and Christian youngsters seeking guidance in a difficult world of moral pollution. This must wait until I have more leisure time (D.V.) to be told.

But as I pause on the uplands of life's experience and take a retrospective look, I am filled with a deep sense of gratitude to the Lord for making use of a worthless wretch like me. God has taken up an insecure, diminutive, colour-blind, uneducated young man with a smouldering resentment against life because of a skin disease, and has fitted him for, and placed him in, a strategic position in His service.

God could quite easily have chosen someone with a more commanding appearance, a better education and with more articulate powers of speech. But our ways are not God's ways. He "hath chosen the foolish things of the world to confound the wise; ... the weak things of the world to confound the things which are mighty; and base things of the world, and things which are despised, hath God chosen, yea, and things which are not, to bring to nought things that are." (1 Cor.1:27-28).

Robert Murray McCheyne has expressed this truth well, "It is not so much a great talent, or knowledge that God blesses, as likeness to Himself. Therefore love, Divine love for God and man, and entire dependence upon the power of the Holy Spirit are the great essentials."

Perhaps a young Christian reader is disturbed because he feels he is not so well equipped as others to serve God. My earnest plea to you is that you'll make the following your life's motto, "Know Him and make Him known." You may indeed look upon yourself as a one-talent believer. Never forget that when you stand before the

Judgment Seat of Christ, your services will be reviewed, and you will be rewarded solely on the basis of the way you have used the gifts (be they many or few) that God has given you. God is prepared to use you for His Glory if you will let Him. In fact, "He is able to do exceedingly abundantly above all that we ask or think, according to the power that worketh in us." (Eph.3:20). This may not mean for you a place of prominence but remember that prominence now is no guarantee of prominence in Eternity and the same can be said about obscurity.

Someone has said, "God is looking for a man, or woman, whose heart will be always set on Him, and who will trust Him for all He desires to do. God is eager to work more mightily now than He ever has through any soul. The clock of the centuries points to the eleventh hour. The world is waiting yet to see what God can do through a consecrated soul. Not the world alone, but God Himself is waiting for one, who will be more fully devoted to Him than any who have ever lived; who will be willing to be nothing that Christ may be all; who will grasp God's own purposes; and taking His humility and His faith, His love and His power, will, without hindering, continue to let God do exploits. There is no limit to what God can do with a man, provided he does not touch the glory."

How eager we all should be to ask the question, "Lord, what wilt Thou have me to do?" How ready we should be to respond to the instructions "Whatsoever He saith unto you do it." And when life's little day of service is over may our joy be full in the knowledge that we have, at least in a measure, obeyed the exhortation: "Whatsoever thy hand findeth to do, do it with thy might."

# Update to 'Love Lifted Me'

When a reprint of 'LOVE LIFTED ME' was deemed worthwhile, the publishers kindly arranged for the following pages to be added to include events subsequent to 1985

An event affording me great personal joy was the conversion of my mother for whom we had prayed for over 30 years. Sad to say, it took the murder of my youngest brother to break her resistance and bring her to the Lord in repentance.

As for Grace and me, we have been serving the Lord in various parts of the West Indies since 1985, having been commended to full-time work by the Assembly in Portessie, Scotland.

When Religious Studies became an examinable subject in Scottish Schools my position in Buckie High became untenable. I could not, with a clear conscience, teach 'World Religions' and give young pupils the impression that Islam and Hinduism, for example, were on a par with the living faith of Christianity.

After much waiting upon the Lord for definite guidance, and asking Him to repeat for us what took place in Acts 13:1-3, we were approached by the elders (who knew nothing about our exercise) and commended to the work.

Our first location was the densely populated valley of Diego Martin, situated 5 miles from Port

205

of Spain, Trinidad. It was a great privilege to help sisters Annie and Eileen Spencer in the running of Bryn Mawr School which nestles in the lush greenery of the slopes of Petit Valley. What a joy it was to teach the Word of God each day to those lovely well-behaved children from different backgrounds. The school also provided a bridge to many homes. Frequently I found myself in a Hindu or Muslim home enquiring about a sick pupil. Concern for the child plus an in-depth knowledge of their religion, invariably enabled me to enter (with sensitivity) into constructive dialogue with the family concerned. We still remember, with great affection, the many friendships that were formed, and especially the young lives that were touched for God during our brief time at Bryn Mawr, whose noble motto is 'God First'.

At that time there were three missionary couples from the UK, one couple from Guyana and a national couple working full-time in Trinidad and Tobago. We had sweet fellowship with them all. Conferences and special meetings brought the saints together from all over Trinidad and the beautiful twin island of Tobago.

Along with others who shared our vision, we had the unspeakable joy of seeing an Assembly planted in the heart of Diego Martin. In this narrow valley, home to some 40,000 souls, Danny and Audrey Ussher had worked hard before moving south, Danny leaving his portable-hall to be used for Gospel outreach. It was in this hall that the saints gathered on May 11th 1986 to break bread for the first time in the newly planted Assembly. Representatives from a number of Assemblies were there to share our joy on that memorable occasion. Regular reports assure me that they are making good progress. Growth is such that a larger hall is required. They have commended their own full-time worker and maintain an outreach work in the surrounding districts.

Can God still open prison doors? Indeed He can! My application to visit the local prison was turned down. Only if a prisoner invited me would I get in but I didn't know anyone who would do so. But the Lord did. When I had to attend the Hospital for treatment for kidney-stones, I had some interesting opportunities to witness for the Lord in the large waiting-room. One afternoon a man in hand-cuffs was escorted in by two armed guards. His chest was bound in bandages. He chose to sit beside me and I started to witness to him. When I quoted John 3:16 his face lit up and he told me that he had heard these words whilst in prison and couldn't get them out of his head. When he had asked a prisoner if he knew what they meant the man stabbed him through his chest puncturing his lung in the process. Hence the reason for being in hospital. The guards sat and listened as I simply unfolded the story of redeeming love to this anxious enquirer. When I had finished, he asked me to visit him and his friends in prison. They were all from Guyana and were Hindus. God had indeed opened the way for us to commence a most fruitful prison ministry! Grace and I visited them on a regular basis and one by one they were brought from the darkness of Hinduism into the glorious Light of Salvation. Prisoners still, but now liberated from spiritual bondage.

Mr Harris, the prison Superintendent, called me into his office to find out what had happened to these men. He told me that prisoners often turn to 'religion' as a last resort, hoping somehow to get released. It was known as the 'Jail-house Conversion Syndrome'. When the sentence is given their religious interest vanishes. He had seen these men placed on 'Death-row' awaiting execution. There their faith had become stronger and fellow-prisoners and guards sought their help for personal problems. "Such is the power of the Gospel" I told Mr Harris.

I was quite emotional, meeting them for the first time after hearing them being sentenced to death for murder. "Don't be upset brother Charles", said Jainarine, "for the moment they put the noose around my neck and the trap-door opens, I will go into the presence of the Lord". I took brother Morris from Guyana in to speak to them because he knew their culture well. Afterwards I asked him what he thought, and with his usual beaming smile he replied, "Dear brother Charles, these men are soundly saved!"

Mr Rowberry, a dear family friend who, along, with his dear wife Grace, has served the Lord among Hindus in India for many years, wrote to encourage the men. A copy of one reply was sent to us, and an extract from it reads:

"I am now 31 years of age and all my life I

never was exposed to the kind of love that
these people has shown me. The Geddes
family has become more than just friends to
me. Because of them I am a happy man on
'Death-row'. Can you believe that? Someone
being happy in a place like this? Yes I am! I
was guided to a caring and loving God Who
sent His Son to die for my sins..."

We were sorry to hear that their request to be
baptised in prison was turned down, but I assured
them that the Lord would take 'the will for the
deed'.

Jainarine's wife had ignored his letters since
his arrest. He asked me to write to her to explain
what had happened to him. What do you write to
the mother of two children whose husband is on
'Death-row'? My letter brought a negative
response from a very bitter woman, full of doubts
and fears about the future, with children having
to endure taunts at school about their father being
a murderer. Our daughter Charlyn consented to
write to her and made a point of remembering the
children's birthdays etc. The following is an
extract from a letter that Kumarie finally wrote
to Charlyn:

"I must tell you that I have start going to
Church—not only going to Church but I have
accept Jesus Christ as my personal Saviour. I
am most thankful to you for inspiring me
about Christ's love. Somehow I find myself
thirsty for more of His knowledge. I wish I

knew the Bible well for I now start loving
God and my life has start being peaceful. I
know that I am not alone any more. I know
there is One Who truly love me."

We were so happy for Kumarie and her
children and also for Charlyn, for hers was indeed
the unspeakable joy of leading, by kind words and
deeds, a poor lost soul along the road that leads to
Christ. Assembly believers in Guyana were
contacted and they take an interest in this family.
Several relatives of the three men have written to
me inviting me to visit them in Guyana with the
Word of God.

Prison waiting-rooms can be sad and sometimes
emotional places, requiring a sympathetic ear
and a large heart if one seeks to witness. One
elderly lady sat in obvious anguish, wringing her
hands and trying to keep back the tears. Her son
apparently couldn't face the misery of a life-
sentence and all he wanted her to bring was a
razor-blade to enable him to end it all.

Prison work can also bring disappointments.
Basdeo made a profession of faith in the Lord and
I was gladly prepared to grant him the little
favour he'd asked, that was to visit his mother-in-law
to seek her forgiveness on his behalf and to ask her to
bring his children to visit him. Only then did he
tell me that he had murdered his wife! When I
arrived at the address in San Juan, I was soon
surrounded by what seemed every Indian in the
neighbourhood. I didn't like their menacing
expressions when I mentioned Basdeo. A sari-

clad old lady was brought to me and I gave her the message. She thanked me most graciously for coming, but with an air of sadness told me that he had killed her beautiful daughter, and his request was out of the question.

Basdeo's reaction on my next visit proved only too well how empty his profession had been and I'd learned a lesson about granting favours too readily. One also learns to cope with those whose profession of faith is immediately followed by the revealing request—"Now can you spare me a few dollars?"

Climbing the steep slopes enclosing the valley of Diego Martin is physically demanding (and the primitive sewage, not at all pleasant sometimes!) Tract distribution is therefore confined mainly to the houses on the valley floor. I decided to concentrate on the more neglected little shacks dotted around the hill-sides. There, unseen from the valley floor, we had a few strange encounters. Once I suddenly came upon a large circle of people, squatting on the ground with eyes closed, totally oblivious to my presence. Not a head moved. Not an eye-lid fluttered. My few words of introduction were ignored so I placed a few tracts on a bench nearby and was glad to leave the eerie silence of the strange scene. Suddenly a piercing scream filled the air. A female voice shrieked the most appalling blasphemies and continued until I was well out of sight. Another cult made a practice of raking the soil around their squalid meeting place. A Pentecostal lady nearby warned me that they scooped up the foot-prints of unwary

passers-by and used them for evil purposes. Of
course you come across some very fine Christians
as well who seek to serve the Lord according to the
light they have.

What do you do when you come across a woman,
heavily pregnant, with a number of naked
children around her? Due to lack of hygiene, they
are badly affected by scabies. Their 'home' is an
old abandoned hut well away from a water and
electricity supply. Do you pretend you didn't see
them? Do you salve your conscience by telling
yourself that you were not out to do social work,
and anyway she no doubt was responsible for the
predicament? I felt unable to do more tract
distribution until I had built a small house for
them near a water and electricity supply, provided
medication to heal their bodies, and with help
from the Homeland, clothed their naked bodies.
All done of course in the Name of the Lord Jesus.

Our last seven months in Trinidad were spent
in Belmont where a flat was provided for us by the
kindly saints of the Belmont Assembly. The Lord
heard our prayers the very week we were to be
made homeless! Visiting the Fairhaven Home
next door to see the elderly saints and share in the
Devotional Services afforded us great joy.

The hillsides of Belmont and Lavantille now
became our 'parish'. But each day I would look
down on the ominous George St. and Nelson St.
area of notorious East Port of Spain. Several
brethren had warned me to keep away from this
dangerous district, where grimy tenements
sweltered in their own filth each day under a

tropical sun, and housed many unsavoury characters. The Lord had however given His command, "Go ye into all the world and preach the Gospel to EVERY creature" (Mark 16:15). This settled the matter for me. EVERY creature must include those living in this veritable 'concrete jungle'. Until the day we left Trinidad, this was where we worked for God. Each day I carried a case of booklets suitable for all age groups and knocked on the doors of the tenements. (These booklets were provided by Mr and Mrs Dennis Clifford, England and proved invaluable, being of very high quality.)

The visible evidence of man when totally given over to sin and Satan was everywhere, but I will not dwell on the sights, sounds and smells of such an unpalatable environment. Rather, I wish to describe two amazing individuals whose courage and faith rose above their surroundings. Imagine my surprise to come to a nicely polished door with gleaming brass handles! The immediate corridor area was scrupulously scrubbed in contrast to the general surroundings. An elderly Christian lady responded to my knock. This dear smiling child of God had lived alone for many years (by choice or otherwise she didn't say). Bad enough by day to live there, but no doubt far worse by night.

Another lady had been concerned about the moral and spiritual welfare of the children. She decided to start a Sunday School, using the basement of a tenement. She had 200 names of children wanting to come. She couldn't teach herself but had been praying for someone to help.

She was so disappointed when I told her we couldn't accept her invitation to take over her ready-made Sunday School, due to our forth-coming departure from Trinidad.

Carrying a heavy case was proving a problem, so I thought the solution would be to find a central location and store brother Clifford's boxes of booklets in a tenement basement. This would facilitate distribution. With considerable difficulty, I finally got a brother to transport a number of boxes for me in his car. Approaching a motley group of men in varying stages of intoxication, I asked the brother to stop. With a distinct look of apprehension he warned me that if I landed in any trouble he would immediately take off. I'd hardly addressed the group when a massive man asked me if I came from Scotland and if I'd ever been in Aberdeen. When I told him I once lived there, he draped his tattooed arms around me in a friendly bear-hug. Apparently he had been a seaman and his ship had docked in Aberdeen. My nervous, wide-eyed escort thought the worst. To him the day of my demise had arrived and only my reassuring gestures that all was well prevented him from making a speedy getaway.

It transpired that the storage of boxes of books was out of the question without getting permission from a certain 'Peppy Joe'. He came on the scene and listened to my problem. He told me that vandals would destroy the books if they were stored in the basement. He invited me to store them in his apartment nearby. His own children would help to distribute them to their young friends. Only later did I learn that Peppy was a gang-leader and that he, along with several other supportive gang-leaders, controlled the whole district. This was, to use their terms, their 'turf'. My acceptance by Peppy Joe meant that I was free to move around the tenements without molestation. I often wondered why I was treated with the utmost courtesy by the shadowy figures who huddled in the dimly-lit stairways smoking 'pot'. I had been mugged a few times in other areas (once when Grace was with me). Only once did this happen in Peppy Joe's area. Some of his friends got to hear that my watch had been stolen. When I described the assailants and where it had happened, I was told to return the next day around lunch-time. When I did so my watch was handed back to me. I didn't have it long after that however.

"TEN MURDERS IN ONE MONTH!" Such were the chilling headlines in the Trinidad 'Evening News' on Monday December 7th 1987. The full-page report began—"a wave of killings has gripped East Port of Spain and residents have asked 'Who's next'?" One afternoon during this spate of killings I placed my watch on a shelf and had a shower. Grace was working in the kitchen nearby. Afterwards I locked the front door, padlocked the gate and set off to post a letter. Returning fifteen minutes later, I learned that someone had climbed over the wall, entered through the unlocked back door, and stolen several items within a few feet of Grace. We dread to think what would have happened had she turned round and confronted the intruder.

"Peppy's in hospital!" Close to tears, the speaker gave a gory account of a gang fight that left Peppy in a critical condition. The 'Mirror' newspaper dated February 26th 1988 carried the whole story on the front page. "GANG WARFARE IS BACK", screamed the headlines and went on: "Gang warfare has made a terrible come-back in Port of Spain and one of the first victims of this resurgence is Alphius Frank, alias 'Peppy Joe'! Severely cut by cutlasses, he was now in hospital along with other casualties. The report went on: "Friends of the wounded men have sworn revenge on the King's Boy gang, and already four different street gangs have jumped into the fray."

As we were due to leave Trinidad that very day, I rushed to the hospital and found the poor man in a dreadful condition. I pleaded with him to accept the Lord as his Saviour, to no avail. He felt too far gone as a sinner for God to save him. He expressed a hope that his children would 'go the right way'. He thanked me for coming into the tenements with the Word of God and assured me that I was the only one who had done so in recent years. Although he survived his injuries, we learned later that he was shot dead in another gang fight. As one sister put it, "He lived by the gun and died by the gun." As for the three men in prison, their sentences were commuted to life imprisonment.

Leaving the land of colour, Carnival, calypso, cricket and, sad to say, crime, we were redirected by the Lord to Aruba (part of the 'ABC' islands of

Aruba, Bonaire and Curacao, which lie about 17 miles off the coast of Venezuela). Aruba is virtually devoid of arable land—a dry, hot, waterless, rocky island. All water comes from the sea via a massive desalination plant. It has a large oil-refinery which was attacked by German submarines during the war.

Four languages are used—Dutch, Spanish, English and Papiamento. There are about 65,000 local people with up to a million tourists coming each year. Aruba is a strong-hold of Romanism (82% being RC) but the Dutch Reformed Church is quite strong too. There are many cults and the small evangelical influence (for the most part) hold to the 'falling-away doctrine'. The small Assembly had an unusual beginning.

In 1938 the late Mr McCune of N. Ireland joined a recruiting ship which was taking hundreds of migrant workers from various islands to work in the giant Lago Oil Refinery, located near San Nicolas in Aruba. Brother McCune was deeply concerned about the moral dangers facing these men (some from the Assemblies) who were leaving behind the restraining influences of home and family. Arriving in Aruba, he gathered the believers together and an Assembly was planted. There were over 60 in fellowship at one time, but the numbers have dwindled to a mere handful today—mostly elderly. This was the situation when Grace and I arrived as the first resident missionaries from the Assemblies.

Getting into Aruba was fraught with problems

that only the Lord could solve for us. At one point the Chief Immigration Officer ordered me out of the island within 3 hours or be put in prison as an illegal immigrant. I neither had a return ticket to Scotland nor any means at hand to buy one. (I came to Aruba with a return ticket to Venezuela only.) Moreover, Grace was in the process of joining me. My claims that the Minister of Justice knew all about my application to reside in Aruba, made the Officer curse and blaspheme God's Name, shout that he alone decided who came into Aruba and who went out and that I'd better be on the afternoon plane or else!

I was almost sick and my mind was in a whirl. I sat outside and prayed for the Lord to undertake for me. A thought entered my mind to go to the Minister of Justice and explain my problem. Not doubting for a moment the Officer's boast, I hoped to be given an extra day or two to settle my affairs. Normally it is impossible to see the Minister's Secretary, far less himself, without an appointment. The two security men weren't slow to tell me so when I approached the impressive building. After much persuasion, to at least try, they 'phoned from their desk, and to their great surprise the Secretary came down. A greater surprise was still to come. After listening to my problem she asked me to wait. Lo and behold! the Minister himself came down and took me aside. I can remember exactly what I said to him that day, "Mr Croes, I came into your island with dignity to preach the Gospel and serve the Lord. All I'm asking for are a few days to settle my affairs and leave with dignity." I then told him about being ordered out of the island.

The man placed his hand on my shoulder. "Mr Geddes", he said, "I too am a born-again Christian. You will stay in Aruba for as long as you want." The only man who could have helped me was not only in his office, not only was prepared to see me (against all custom) but above all was a fellow-believer. The Chief Immigration Officer was removed from his post a few weeks later!

Feelings of isolation in a pioneer work can be almost overwhelming. One visiting brother commented, "You would need to be called to live in a place like this." Starting from scratch we were forced to create new avenues of service, (apart from the usual Assembly meetings). This led to prison and hospital visitation work, preaching weekly in two Senior Citizen's groups, giving free lessons in English to immigrants and visiting day-care centres. Tract distribution led to Eddie getting saved—the first Arubian saved through Assembly out-reach. A life-long RC, he trusted the Lord after reading a 'Via' magazine I gave him. Edward Jaminson of Belfast sent tracts in plastic envelopes for Deep Sea Evangelism. The Gulf Stream carried them along the coast-line of several Central American countries. During the English lessons, some young people from Haiti got saved. The Assembly meetings did not appeal to them, however, and they preferred the company of young people along with the 'excitement' of the Pentecostals.

Sonya had been abused as a child as she moved

from one foster home to another. She grew up hating authority and with very low self-esteem. When I told her that I wanted to introduce her to my best Friend she showed some interest. She broke down when I told her how much He loved her. She accepted a copy of my book and promised to read it. Before the week was out she was saved. Instead of tearing the hair from the warders heads, she was (to their amazement) offering to give them a hairdo. The change in the behaviour of Sonya—once viewed as completely "incorrigible", was a wonderful testimony to the transforming power of the Gospel.

Few places in this world can rival Grenada (the "Isle of Spice") for unspoiled beauty. The grandeur of lofty mountains covered with rain-forests, bustling street-markets selling locally-grown fruit, and the breath-taking view of the harbour at St George's, are but a few of the sights etched on my memory. How different from the flat, sterile barrenness of Aruba, and yet the spiritual needs of both are exactly alike and I was in Grenada on a month's visit as an evangelist, not as a tourist.

Each morning I set off early to spend the whole day handing out tracts and the "Via" magazine. Each night, apart from Saturdays, I preached the Gospel in Gospel Halls and hired schools. We had some wonderful meetings and it was good to see a unity of purpose among the believers with the assemblies rallying to support one another.

The Principal of "Happy Hill" Secondary School invited me to address the whole school and give my testimony. I felt a real burden as I spoke through the loudspeaker in the middle of the school courtyard, and brought before the large crowd of teenagers the great Truth found in Proverbs chapter one—"The fear of the Lord is the beginning of knowledge". Later, one pupil pushed her way through the dispersing crowd and tearfully told me that the message had deeply affected her.

I left Grenada spiritually enriched by the sweet fellowship of God's dear people. I was deeply moved by the kind words of gratitude expressed by various speakers at my "farewell meeting" and the insistence that I return as soon as possible. I often pray that suitable political leaders will be raised up, to harness the existing assets of such a beautiful island for the well-being of its hard-working, friendly people.

A month in St Vincent followed a similar pattern. Open-air preaching yielded some fruit as did daily visits to homes, market places and the local hospital.

When I returned to Aruba in early 1996 it was to find that our house had been looted in our absence. The loss of material possessions was nothing compared with the wanton destruction of mail. Thankfully a kindly neighbour salvaged some.

Determined not to succumb to discouragement, and thereby give the enemy the victory, I immediately set off to circulate portions of Scripture in a number of Caribbean islands. Along with fellow-workers from America, we visited as many schools as possible in Dominica,

Barbados and Puerto Rico. Gospels of John were
given to the pupils and New Testaments to the
teachers. Being a former teacher helped to
remove any suspicion regarding our intentions
and I was allowed to address a number of classes.
It was good to meet fellow-workers such as
Dalmar Edwards in Antigua and Mildred Murray
in Barbados. Needless to say, we were kept busy
in both the ministry and gospel.

This trip gave me a good insight into the
different spiritual needs of the assemblies and the
varied social conditions of the islands. The
poverty of rural Dominica was an eye-opener.
Never have I seen so many people going around
barefoot, seeking to eke out a precarious living
growing bananas, and hoping the crop will not be
destroyed by the next passing hurricane. We too
need to pray that the good Seed sown in the hearts
of so many thousands of children will bring forth
fruit for the Glory of God.

# Autumn Years' Reflections

We chose to live in the poorer area of Aruba, known locally as "Chocolate City". As the name suggests, only black people lived there. We were known as "Mr and Mrs Scotland" and were on the best of terms with everyone. The Assembly bus was made available so that the people could have the use of it. The hospital and airport were fifteen miles away, so the bus proved a real asset to them. They openly expressed their surprise that we (their only white neighbours) had chosen to live there. We wanted to reach them for God.

Miss Ethel (our "kindly neighbour" already referred to) became like one of our family. Approaching ninety years of age, she wanted to leave her lovely house and period furniture to us in her will. Although such generosity would no doubt have greatly expanded certain aspects of our work, we declined her offer. She was in good health mentally, had no near relatives, and there were no legal problems. She meant well, but didn't realise we could have been exposed to accusations of covetousness and become the targets of envy in the community. We had to live lives above reproach, in order to serve the Lord effectively. We have a cunning enemy who will do his utmost to destroy the work of God. To safeguard against this, all impressions of the "us and them" attitude of supposed superiority of race and culture had also to be carefully avoided.

It was Miss Ethel who invited me to speak at the Senior Citizens' meetings. A number of members got saved. One case comes to mind.

Monica (also ninety years old) was a staunch life-long Roman Catholic. After each Gospel message I would hear her mutter, "I was born a Catholic and I will die a Catholic!".

One January, however, the lady in charge asked the group, if anything exciting had happened to any of them during the Christmas recess. Monica stood up and addressed the company.

With firm voice she said, "I want you all to know that during the Christmas break I was quite ill. I came to realise that what I believed all my life was wrong. I knew I wasn't ready to die. I knew Mary couldn't take away my sins. Only Jesus could do that. He is the only way to Heaven. He is now my Saviour. You all need to be saved too". Lasting impressions were no doubt made that night.

I can still remember the solemn message the late veteran missionary Bob Leighton gave to the same group. Listening with rapt attention, they drank in every word. He was an old man addressing old people, and that itself carried weight.

Bob had come over from Scotland to spend six weeks with us. He and his dear wife had served the Lord in Cuba, the Bahamas, and latterly Puerto Rico, for fifty years. Although getting on in years and quite deaf, he was still full of spiritual vitality and truly "bringing forth fruit in old age".

One day we heard of six men who had been rescued from shark infested waters ten miles off Aruba. They were in the local hospital and in very poor condition. When Bob heard that they were from the Dominican Republic he immediately suggested that we visit them. We phoned the hospital and were granted permission.

In the hospital the men related how they had paid a crew-member to hide them in an oil-tanker, thinking they were en-route to Puerto Rico. The captain, however, had been given fresh orders to go elsewhere, and the crew-member was afraid to reveal that he had concealed stowaways.

Without food and very little water for nine days, their calls for help were finally heard. They claimed, however, that the callous captain just threw them overboard. They were rescued from certain death by a passing yacht.

I stood aside as our brother conversed with them in Spanish. I understood most of what was said. They were in a dreadful physical condition with ugly blotches all over their skin. Bob asked them where they would now be if thy had perished in the sea.

Emotionally they chorused, "Infierno" (Hell). With deep feeling, this godly man proceeded to present the Gospel to them. I silently prayed as I witnessed a most moving scene. Here were six men snatched from the very jaws of death, now hanging on to his every word. I could see the tears brimming the eyes of some of them.

Suddenly one, in full view of his companions, threw himself down on his knees, as he called on God to save his soul. Our brother appealed to the others with great solemnity to do likewise, but to no avail.

Eventually the man rose from his knees and the joy of his face told its own story. He announced that he was saved.

Brother Bob had a closing prayer and then asked the man who had just risen from his knees.

"And where will you go if you should die tonight?"

The man answered, "Cielo" (Heaven).

They were given names and addresses of some missionaries in the Dominican Republic who were known to Bob.

The Superintendent of the hospital thought that we were sent by the Immigration authorities, otherwise our request to visit the men would have been refused. Had we not come when we did, we would have missed the opportunity, for they were due to fly home that afternoon. Dear brother Bob assured the bewildered Superintendent that we had been sent by a much higher Authority. Going home he said it was worth coming all the way to Aruba for that experience alone. He was a very happy man and he celebrated his 84th birthday with us.

Oscar had been brain-washed for years by the "Jehovah Witness" cult (I prefer to call them "Watch tower Witnesses", for such they are). He just could not accept the truth of the Deity of Christ. Now he has been wonderfully saved, and delivered from the bondage of that evil system.

He is employed as a Tourist Information Guide and interacts with many tourists who holiday in Aruba. As he becomes more confident, it is hoped that he will become a true witness for Christ, and will guide many of them on to the Highway to Heaven.

Gurandy lives a few doors from the Gospel Hall in Aruba. His sisters had been in our Sunday school, and, along with their mother, had got saved, baptised, and come into Assembly fellowship. I listened to their individual testimonies in their home.

Gurandy sat in a corner with his head bowed. I asked him why he hadn't trusted the Lord as they had done, and he remained silent. Without putting any pressure on him (for I have a great fear of false professions) I told him what would happen when the Lord returned.

What a joy it was to see him come on his own to hear me preach the Gospel that evening. He sat right at the front and told me afterwards that he had accepted the Lord as his Saviour in his own little room after my visit.

Regarding "false professions" I can remember the concern of a dear brother in Union Island. He had no time for "easy believism", the raising of hands at the end of a lengthy, emotional appeal, or the reciting parrot-fashion of a set prayer. These are his words, "Brother Charles, for years we have been lamenting over the increasing numbers of backsliders in the assemblies. I think we should now address the real problem and that is whether or not they were saved at all". One has to admit that the light-hearted, emotional nature of some of the West Indians can pose a problem. We can only say with absolute certainty - "The foundation of the God standeth sure, having this seal, the Lord knoweth them that are His".

Like Monica, Elizabeth was a Staunch Roman Catholic. She was dying of AIDS through no fault of her own. Her unfaithful husband had infected her. He had died, and now she had only a week or two to live. Her three lovely children would be left without parents and be brought up in an R.C orphanage. I'd heard that she was very bitter. She had refused to see visitors and wanted to be left alone with her thoughts. I decided to try. On one of my regular hospital visits I entered the little side ward she was in, all by herself. She seemed to be asleep, so I drew a chair close to her bed and quietly said, "Elizabeth, I want to introduce you to my best Friend", (my favourite opening gambit).

She slowly opened her weary eyes and focussed them on me, and then gradually looked around the ward, presumably looking for my Friend.

"My best Friend is the Lord Jesus", I continued. "He wants to be your best Friend too", I said.

There was no response, so I tried another approach. I reminded her of the day she got married. Her husband-to-be had been asked if he would take her to be his lawful wedded wife and he had replied in the affirmative. I pointed out that she too had been asked a similar question and had given a similar reply. They had received each other. They now belonged to each other.

I then slowly read from John ch1 verses 11 and 12. "He came unto His own and His own received Him not, but as many as received Him, to them gave He power to become the sons of God, even to them that believe on His name".

"Elizabeth", I said, almost choking with emotion,

"Religion can't help you. You need a relationship with the Lord Jesus. I believe that God is near today and is saying to you, 'Will you, Elizabeth take My Son to be your Lord and Saviour?' What is your answer going to be?"

Before I could say another word, from somewhere deep within her wasted, skeletal frame, I heard a cry that must have echoed along the corridor - "I will! I will! I will!" Within a few days Elizabeth was at Home with the Lord.

Hebrews chapter 11 verse 32 states, "And what shall I more say? For the time would fail me to tell…".

I must give all praise and glory to God for some specific and timely answers to prayer (some perhaps mundane but some certainly memorable). Some, like the opening of prison doors and the gaining favour with gang leader Peppie Joe in Trinidad, I've mentioned. I've referred to the timely intervention of the Minister of Justice in Aruba.

We can add to that the almost last minute provision of the missionary flat in Belmont, Trinidad, preventing us from being made homeless. Also the arrival at night of a Dr Bontierre asking me if I could use certain medication for my kidney - stone problem. It was surplus stock and it was exactly what I desperately needed!

In answer to prayer, on two separate occasions, tracts and booklets arrived by post, (one by John Stubbs and another by Douglas Mowat). Radio ministry had brought certain enquiries requiring careful thought, and they just met the need perfectly.

On one occasion, we returned to Trinidad (after being home to Scotland for key-hole surgery). We were met by the Immigration Authorities who told us that our work permit had been cancelled in our absence. We would not be allowed to enter the country without on-going tickets. This we didn't have and had no means of getting without money at that late hour!

Weary after the long flight, Grace and I felt like criminals as scores of curious passengers looked on. Too traumatized to think properly, and fully expecting to be held in some form of detention, we could only lift up our hearts to God in prayer.

The quick thinking of a missionary who was there to meet us provided the solution. He found a travel agent (from where, I still don't know), who was not only sympathetic, but also willing to provide us with the expensive tickets that we required. He was prepared to trust us to delay the payment until the following day! God had once again proved to be "a very present help in trouble" (Psalm 46:1).

Once I found myself stranded in an airport in St Lucia. The brother I was expecting to put me up for the night until the flight next morning to St Vincent, hadn't turned up, and efforts to contact him failed. Already tired and miserable, I certainly did not relish the prospect of spending the night there alone.

Hour after hour I sat with my luggage, until darkness fell. One by one the lights went out, as the staff left. Eventually, a pick-up on its own, remained in the car-park. To stretch my legs I strolled around it. I noticed the Gospel texts displayed on the window. I complimented the owner, who was now approaching.

We exchanged greetings, and a brief discussion brought to light my dilemma. He put my case into his truck and I thought he was heading for his home. He drove me to a nearby large hotel instead. He turned a deaf ear to my protests. He told the receptionist to give me a meal right away and provide me with the best room. He told her to make sure that I was given an English breakfast in the morning, all at his expense! Then he promised to pick me up in time to catch my plane next day.

The receptionist asked me how I knew Mr Harris (for that was his name) She informed me that he was the Chief Custom's Officer at the airport. When I told her that we had only met five minutes earlier her eyes bulged. When I declared that we had the same Father, they bulged even further. Mr Harris was black, as she herself was. I explained of course that God was our Father and that the Lord Jesus was our Saviour.

True to his word, Mr Harris came just as I was finishing a hearty breakfast. I had slept well in a most comfortable bed. It was certainly the largest I'd ever seen. I'd fallen asleep that night rejoicing in the faithfulness of God. But what an anti-climax at the airport! It was the wrong one! My on-going flight was from another airport further north. The travel agent had forgotten to tell me. By this time it was too late to catch it. I was due to speak at a Conference in St. Vincent that day!

Again Mr Harris came to my rescue. He insisted that I be given a standby seat, telling the girl at the desk that I had very important business to attend to that day. I will never forget the kindness of that fine Christian gentleman.

Was it a mere coincidence that he was the last

person to leave the airport and that I should decide to stroll round his truck and spot the texts just as he was about to leave? I certainly don't think so.

Poverty and crime are close companions. We saw this in Trinidad and also St. Vincent where we stayed for an extended period at the request of the Elders of the Kingstown assembly. An apartment above the Gospel Hall was made available to us and we saw considerable fruit for our labours. Sadly, Grace had to return to Scotland to attend to family matters.

Handing out tracts in Central Kingstown

Central Kingstown, with its street vendors and massive multi-storey indoor market simply swarmed with people from all over the island. It was an ideal place to have open-air meetings, using the excellent loud-speaking equipment supplied by the brethren. There is a hunger for the Word there, rarely seen in other places. Eternity alone will reveal the full impact made.

When darkness fell, the very air seemed fraught with danger, however. Security guards patrolled the city streets to protect the commercial premises. As our apartment had a balcony providing a bird's-eye view of the city centre, and all the nefarious activity going on, we saw human nature at its worst. Thankfully, the brethren had carried out extensive burglar-proofing, with heavy iron bars over windows and doors, so that one felt safe.

It was from this balcony that I got a clear view of William (a security guard) getting gunned down by two robbers. I'd witnessed to him many times as he guarded the petrol-station across from the hall. Apparently he was a backslider and had a "common-law" wife.

Scantily attired as I was (being ready for bed) I rushed across to assist him. Blood was everywhere. I was soon covered with it as I tried to stem the flow from a gun-shot wound in his chest. Several on-lookers stood nearby but offered no aid. Thankfully, one of my own Bible-class pupils (no doubt led of God) drew in for petrol, unaware of the situation. He sped William to the emergency unit at the hospital. It was touch and go for him for three days, but he finally pulled through.

He came back to the Lord and started attending the meetings in the Gospel Hall. He wanted to get properly married there, with me officiating. I was due to come home on furlough, however, so that wasn't possible.

I was told later that the onlookers had remained at a safe distance because of the fear of AIDS. With so much blood around they didn't want to put themselves at risk (an indication of how rife the disease is in St. Vincent and some other West Indian islands. The Carnival festival doesn't help).

Wesley was another back-slider. Saved in the Kingstown Sunday School, he had shown great promise. He went to Trinidad, however, and backslid. He was now suffering from AIDS and had come home to die (still in his teens). Wracked with guilt, he was afraid to meet God. Wendy, his mother, was broken-hearted and tearfully described his mental anquish and agony of soul, groaning night and day as he wasted away. She begged me to come and help him.

What I saw lying on her couch was a "living corpse", with large eyes bulging out of a shrunken face. I felt out of my comfort zone as I heard his pathetic groans. His poor mother could bear no more and left the room.

"Wesley", I said, "God doesn't condone the mess you have made of your life, but His love for you is unconditional and unchanging. His love doesn't ebb and flow like ours. He can't possibly love you any more than He does now. He will never love you any less." His groaning gradually stopped, but he said nothing. I quietly unfolded to him the wonderful truth of God's matchless love.

A few days later his mother came to tell me that Wesley had died. She had never seen him so happy as he breathed his last, with a hymn-book in hand, trying his best to sing "Jesus loves me this I know, for the Bible tells me so." The awareness of God's love had lifted Wesley from the depths of depression and the loss of assurance caused by his back-sliding.

Shortly afterwards I was held up by two men, one wielding a gun. The gun-man stood in front of me and threatened to pull the trigger if I didn't co-operate. It was a dark, wet night, with few people about.

In the dim light of the street lamp, the gun had a plastic look about it. I foolishly laughed in his face and told him that I didn't think it was a real gun. This, of course was just a nervous reaction, as I tried to stall in order to gather my confused wits together.

Snarling with rage, he rammed the gun barrel full force into my stomach, telling me not to mess around with them. By this time his accomplice had taken my wallet and apartment keys.

Recovering somewhat, I told them that I was a servant of God and that He would deal with them for what they were doing to me. The sad tone of the gun-man surprised me as he answered, "I know He will".

I proceeded to tell them that God loved them and had sent His Son to die for them. I remember them asking me where I preached. I told them that they may have heard me down at the market.

Before they left with only fifty Caribbean dollars for their efforts, (no ring, no watch) they told me to take them to my car. I told them I didn't have a car so they retreated into the shadows and disappeared. Before they left I called after them, "And when you get saved, bring back my fifty dollars!" They both gave a hearty laugh.

I decided to report the robbery to the police. As I gave my report, a man in an evening suit sat listening at an adjoining table. With him were two ladies in their evening gowns. They were quietly sobbing. They had been at a party, and had also been robbed earlier by the same two men. They had lost a lot of money and jewellery.

When the man heard me relate how I had laughed into the gun-man's face, he couldn't restrain himself.

"Are you crazy?" he asked, "that was a 9mm semi-automatic revolver! I'm a plain-clothes policeman and I should know, for we use them all the time!"

The police drove me to the hospital to get medical help for my bruised stomach. They also needed a medical report in case the men were eventually caught. The charge of assault would have to be added in my case. They hoped that I would attend any future trial as a witness, and they gave me a "To whom it may concern" letter with that in view.

That same week the newspaper had a list of the "most wanted" criminals. I recognized my assailant's face right away.

"Unless he has a twin brother, that's the man", I told the police. The Head of C.I.D unfolded a grim account of the man's record. Included were several murders. Only three week's earlier, a businessman had been robbed, along with a lady friend, by him as they sat in their car. Then they were forced at gun-point to drive the robbers to a remote secluded bay, where their get-away speed-boat was moored.

The man was shot, and they buried him in the sand. His lady-friend was also shot, but the killers must have been disturbed, and she survived to tell the tale.

Glancing through my report before him, he said, "You should thank your lucky stars you didn't have a car. You wouldn't be here now if you had".

Of course we don't thank any kind of stars, but only the One who cares for His own.

That care was demonstrated to me one memorable night. After checking the double locks on the door on my apartment I prepared for bed. After a long day out in the oppressive heat, I was usually ready to drop off to sleep. (This was before my kidney malfunction had become a major problem).

This night, however, I just couldn't sleep. I got up and proceeded to write letters. Midnight came but I seemed fresher than ever. Most unusual! Taking a book by Sir Robert Anderson, I propped myself up on the bed. As the city slept, I passed the hours reading.

It was about four o'clock when I thought I saw the door begin to slowly open. There was only one door to my bedroom and the windows were burglar-proofed. Humanly speaking, I was totally defenceless and virtually trapped.

My brain just froze. The door just couldn't open on its own! But it was opening ever so slowly, reaching 90 degrees. The doorway was on the opposite side, out-with my view, so I was totally unaware of what, or who, was on the other side. My brain began to tell me as the seconds ticked by that I was about to confront some kind of demonic apparition. The adrenalin was flowing fast. Without the shadow of a doubt, this was for me the most petrifying experience of my life.

Slowly a hooded shape appeared. A black bearded face peered in my direction and I immediately shouted at the top of my voice "In the name of the Lord Jesus I command you to leave this building!"

Quick as a flash the shape vanished, followed by a series of rumbling sounds. Apart from the bedroom, the house was in darkness. The hall-way switch was beyond my reach, so I had no way of knowing where the intruder was. I decided to preach into the darkness as I stood shivering with the cold and no doubt with fear. It was a "flight or fight" situation, but where could I go? There was nowhere to flee to. I quietly prayed for God's help.

I finally plucked up courage to rush to the switch, to illuminate the apartment. Nobody was there! I had been preaching into empty space! Confusion reigned again as I checked the doors. Everything intact. What was going on here I wondered?

Then I noticed the curtain of the kitchen window wafting in the night air. Someone, somehow, had managed to come into the apartment this way, and I hadn't heard a sound!

The brethren never dreamt that anyone could possibly reach that window so high above the ground, far less be able to climb through it. This man had done so in the dark, without a long ladder, and without making a sound. How it was done still remains a mystery.

The arrow points to the window where the intruder entered

His intention was no mystery, however. He fully expected me to be asleep. The brethren assured me, that he would have finished me off, allowing him to rob the apartment with ease. Apparently cat-burglars were very active in St. Vincent, and life was cheap.

I believe firmly that the Lord had deprived me of sleep that night so I could challenge the intruder. How he survived the leap to the concrete alleyway from such a height in the darkness I don't know. He no doubt thought I was armed and that his own life was in danger. If he had only known!

I relate this incident in detail because it reinforces the importance of the believers at home regularly praying for the missionaries. Remember there are about four hours of a time difference between the U.K and St. Vincent. We had prayer-partners interceding for us during their morning devotions at the very time this drama was unfolding. Needless to say, the window was immediately burglar-proofed!

We are now in the "reflective years" of our earthly pilgrimage. Times tides have changed the patterns on the sands of our life's shore. God's love and protection have remained unchanged, however. The distressing psoriasis disease that plagued my early years and brought me to despair, almost completely cleared up about forty years ago, and thankfully, has not come back. "How good is the God we adore".

We go on short visits now. Last year I spent a month going round our former fields of service. I visited the three prisoners we had led to the Lord in Trinidad in 1986. It was out-with normal visiting hours, but these men had so impressed the prison authorities with their Christian testimony inside prison, that I was granted special permission to visit them. It was a remarkable experience and they were not expecting me. What a difference I saw! In the past they were rough, semi-illiterate men, and had killed a man. Now they were confident, erudite, fluent speakers, quoting the Scriptures with ease and telling with great enthusiasm something of the work they were doing to help their fellow prisoners. Little wonder they are respected within

Jainarine being honoured by the Head of Prisons

the prison and have been officially honoured by the Prison Governor. She even allowed them to be baptized in a special tank within the prison.

The Head of the C.I.D in St. Vincent told me when I went to his office, that the gun-man who had assaulted and robbed me had been shot dead in St. Lucia. He had been caught in the act of robbing people again. My appeals to him and his partner in crime, to give up their awful life-styles and accept the Lord as their Saviour, had obviously fallen on deaf ears. I felt sad, because I'd hoped that he had been apprehended and I could have visited him in prison.

I was able to visit a family in Kingstown whose son I had tried in vain to save from drowning during the first hours of the year 2000. They were so happy to see me. The mother came to the Gospel meeting and promised the Elders that she would come back again. I was pleased to see some fruit during the few Gospel meetings I had during my visit.

The "icing on the cake" of my visit, however, was the wonderful transformation of the "bike man" in Aruba. I'd witnessed for the Lord to Mr King for over twenty years.

He was well known as a local character. All his worldly possessions were tied to an old bike. Every day found him in the square of

Oranjestad. His clothes were shabby, and his shoes tied with string.

After my regular tract distribution I would spend some time with him before getting the bus home. Our discussions sometimes got heated, and he would become verbally abusive. He had examined every cult under the sun, and knew quite a bit about the Bible.

His only shelter was a rough make-shift plastic sheet in the bush. He insisted that rattlesnakes are harmless, and won't touch you if you don't touch them.

Imagine my surprise to hear him call to me from across a busy street! Here he was, smartly dressed in a security officer uniform, working at a major bank. He was so pleased to see me for he had some wonderful news to share. He was now gloriously saved!

Mr King went on to tell me how his verbal abuse (for which he profusely apologized) had just been a front. He had been genuinely searching for the truth and he had considered carefully the Gospel message I brought to him. Unknown to me, he was under deep conviction, and during my absence he had finally accepted the Lord as his Saviour.

He was now gainfully employed and seeking to win others for the Lord. He lived now in a comfortable home (I don't know what happened to the bike!) What a transformation! He was so happy to see me and to thank me for being so patient with him. The Gospel certainly is "the power of God unto salvation to every one that believeth".

And so the work goes on, expanding like the ripples in a pool. My story has been translated into Spanish - "Su Amor Me Levanto", by brother Alves of Venezuela, and widely circulated in Latin America.

The renowned Pacific Garden Mission in Chicago has put it on cassette, and now use it on their radio programme "Unshackled". It is heard in 147 countries in 6 Continents from 1,150 radio outlets in English, Spanish, Arabic, Romanian,

Preparing to broadcast the gospel through radio ministry

Russian and Polish. Listeners are offered further help and free literature. Tapes are sent on request, free of charge, to individuals or evangelistic groups who desire to promote the Gospel, (especially among the young).

I should point out that we have never desired to gain financially from any sales of the book (quite the reverse). Copies have been widely given free to Prisons, Public Libraries, and Deep Sea Missions etc as well as to interested individuals. Sowing the Seed was all that mattered.

A thorough check up at the Edinburgh International Health Centre (courtesy of "Interlink", Glasgow) not surprisingly detected clear symptoms of "post traumatic stress disorder". That's a very small price to pay for the unspeakable privilege of serving the One "Who loved me and gave Himself for me". YES LOVE LIFTED ME!

I have finally to state with profound sincerity that apart from Grace's unfailing support and steadying influence throughout the years, very little would have been accomplished. We have been spared "through many dangers toils and snares" to celebrate our Golden Wedding anniversary and to walk hand in hand into the sunset of life together. To God be all the praise and all the Glory!

Many thanks for taking the time to read my humble story. What God has done for me, He can do for you. If I can be of any help to you, please feel free to write to me. My address is:-

> 14 Doran Drive,
> BUCKIE
> MORAY
> SCOTLAND
> AB56 1DF

Email:- charlesgeddes@hotmail.co.uk